I'M GOING TO BE A DAD: NOW WHAT?

Everything You Need to Know About First-Time Fatherhood

By Craig Baird

I'M GOING TO BE A DAD: NOW WHAT? EVERYTHING YOU NEED TO KNOW ABOUT FIRST-TIME FATHERHOOD

Copyright © 2010 Atlantic Publishing Group, Inc.
1405 SW 6th Avenue • Ocala, Florida 34471 • Phone 800-814-1132 • Fax 352-622-1875
Web site: www.atlantic-pub.com • E-mail: sales@atlantic-pub.com
SAN Number: 268-1250

ISBN-13: 978-1-60138-395-2 ISBN-10: 1-60138-395-2

Library of Congress Cataloging-in-Publication Data

Baird, Craig W., 1980-
  I'm going to be a dad : now what? everything you need to know about first-time fatherhood / by Craig W. Baird.
    p. cm.
  Includes bibliographical references and index.
  ISBN-13: 978-1-60138-395-2 (alk. paper)
  ISBN-10: 1-60138-395-9 (alk. paper)
  1. Fatherhood. 2. Fathers. 3. Father and child. I. Title.
  HQ756.B334 2009
  649'.10242--dc22

                          2009031312

Printed in the United States

PROJECT MANAGER: Erin Everhart • eeverhart@atlantic-pub.com
ASSISTANT EDITOR: Angela Pham • apham@atlantic-pub.com
INTERIOR DESIGN: Antoinette D'Amore • addesign@videotron.ca
COVER & JACKET DESIGN: Jackie Miller • sullmill@charter.net

Printed on Recycled Paper

We recently lost our beloved pet "Bear," who was not only our best and dearest friend but also the "Vice President of Sunshine" here at Atlantic Publishing. He did not receive a salary but worked tirelessly 24 hours a day to please his parents. Bear was a rescue dog that turned around and showered myself, my wife, Sherri, his grandparents Jean, Bob, and Nancy, and every person and animal he met (maybe not rabbits) with friendship and love. He made a lot of people smile every day.

We wanted you to know that a portion of the profits of this book will be donated to The Humane Society of the United States. –*Douglas & Sherri Brown*

The human-animal bond is as old as human history. We cherish our animal companions for their unconditional affection and acceptance. We feel a thrill when we glimpse wild creatures in their natural habitat or in our own backyard.

Unfortunately, the human-animal bond has at times been weakened. Humans have exploited some animal species to the point of extinction.

The Humane Society of the United States makes a difference in the lives of animals here at home and worldwide. The HSUS is dedicated to creating a world where our relationship with animals is guided by compassion. We seek a truly humane society in which animals are respected for their intrinsic value, and where the human-animal bond is strong.

Want to help animals? We have plenty of suggestions. Adopt a pet from a local shelter, join The Humane Society and be a part of our work to help companion animals and wildlife. You will be funding our educational, legislative, investigative and outreach projects in the U.S. and across the globe.

Or perhaps you'd like to make a memorial donation in honor of a pet, friend or relative? You can through our Kindred Spirits program. And if you'd like to contribute in a more structured way, our Planned Giving Office has suggestions about estate planning, annuities, and even gifts of stock that avoid capital gains taxes.

Maybe you have land that you would like to preserve as a lasting habitat for wildlife. Our Wildlife Land Trust can help you. Perhaps the land you want to share is a backyard— that's enough. Our Urban Wildlife Sanctuary Program will show you how to create a habitat for your wild neighbors.

So you see, it's easy to help animals. And The HSUS is here to help.

THE HUMANE SOCIETY
OF THE UNITED STATES.

2100 L Street NW • Washington, DC 20037 • 202-452-1100
www.hsus.org

DEDICATION

To Layla, My Muse

TABLE OF CONTENTS

Chapter 6: The Baby's First Three Months   117

Chapter 7: From Three Months to Two Years 161

Section 3: The Reference Guide 207

Chapter 8: Illnesses and Your Baby   209

Chapter 9: Baby Dangers   227

Chapter 10: Games for the Baby   239

Chapter 11: Being a Father   249

FOREWORD

Fatherhood is a gift handed to us from God. I am truly fortunate to be a dad. *I'm Going to Be a Dad: Now What? Everything You Need to Know about First-Time Fatherhood* begins by taking you through all stages of the mother's pregnancy. Most chapters are punctuated by a conclusion and case study, which adds to the book's completeness. The work discusses ways you can baby proof your home and how to select the correct car seat for your newborn. *I'm Going to be a Dad* offers succinct anecdotes that not only new fathers should know, but also information for first-time mothers.

You will learn how to change your infant's diaper, give your baby a bath, and protect and nurture your new bundle of joy. Page 102 of this book states, "Naturally, since your baby will be falling over a lot, you should go around the house and put padding on all sharp corners. This is especially true in the living room, where you will have to put padding on the tables, shelves, and even on the sides of walls or in doorways." Author Craig Baird does not beat around the bush with this handy book. As a newbie to fatherhood, you are expected to protect and support the mother and child and to be the rock of the family.

To be forewarned is to be forearmed, and by reading *I'm Going to Be a Dad*, expectant fathers will learn that an ounce of prevention is worth a pound of cure. From coping with your partner's pregnancy and choosing the right doctor, to attending the right Lamaze classes, this practical book offers sage advice. Although I am far past my baby-making years, I found the book to be cathartic. It offers a wealth of support for men who need a 101 Fatherhood Instructional Guide.

As a prospective father, what you need to know is contained within these pages. Having a medical background, I found the reference section to be informative and helpful. *I'm Going to Be a Dad* is a fun read, and by soaking up its information, you will become a better father.

This work alerts you to the possible pitfalls of pregnancy, as well as your child's first few years of life. Embrace it! *I'm Going to Be a Dad* reminds us that not all fathers are created equal, and we have a lot to learn and know. The book serves as a life jacket for first-time fathers and does not disappoint.

There are other expectant father books out there, but Baird's *I'm Going to Be a Dad* will keep you turning those pages, hungering and thirsting for more. I am fairly confident that prominent parenting experts would agree with me that this book is a must read for all dads-to-be. Welcome to the world of paternity!

Foreword Author Bio

Dean Tong is a forensic trial consultant, author, speaker, and expert who has worked with contested divorces, custody battles, and abuse cases in 47 states and Canada. A former Board of Adviser to the American Coalition for Fathers and Children, Tong, a father, has been seen on CNN, Court-TV, Dateline, CBS 48 Hours, ABC Prime Time and Dr. Phil. His fourth book, *Children of the Lie,* is due out in 2010. For more information, visit his Web site, **www.DeanTong.com**.

SECTION 1

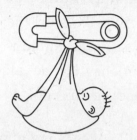

Getting Through the Nine Months

> "You should never say anything to a woman that even remotely suggests that you think she's pregnant unless you can see an actual baby emerging from her at that moment."
>
> - Dave Barry, syndicated humor columnist

So, it has begun. Your partner has given you the big news and your life has been changed forever. Now you are ready to begin preparing for the arrival of a new bundle of joy in nine months. This can be a bit daunting to think about, and your mind may become overloaded with the thoughts of everything that you need to begin preparing. Over the next nine months, there will be some changes in the house and in your partner. By preparing yourself for these changes, they will not be such a shock, and you will be able to manage much more easily.

Through this first section, we will look at all three trimesters that your partner will be going through. Each trimester is going to bring changes, joys, and difficulties. This is all part of the process of bringing a new life into the world, and you are not the first to go through them. Each year, millions of men and women go through the joy of pregnancy, but not all of them are able to prepare like you are by reading this book.

Overall, the section will cover being a father, from the first day that you find out about the pregnancy to the birth of the baby that is going to change your life; you will learn everything you need to know about helping your partner, the baby, and yourself to get through these next nine months as easily as possible.

Today is the beginning of a whole new life for you, one filled with excitement and love.

So, let us begin!

CHAPTER 1

The First Trimester

"Making a decision to have a child — it's momentous.
It is to decide forever to have your heart go walking
around outside your body."

-Elizabeth Stone, author

The shock of finding out that you are going to be a father has worn off. Now the realization of what is ahead has hit you. It may seem daunting to realize what you will have to do over the next three months, but it can be easy to prepare yourself for the changes ahead.

Throughout the first three months, you will take steps that will be very important down the road, including choosing a doctor, changing your diet, and watching for the signs of a miscarriage. Aspects like the first doctor's appointment, ultrasound, and coping with morning sickness are also all vital factors in preparing for being a father.

As the father of the baby, you have a special task ahead of you. While your significant other is carrying the baby, you are helping her out to make things easier for her. This is going to be a long nine months for her, but you can make it easier, and it all begins in the first trimester.

Understanding Trimesters

First things first: We will address the trimesters. Pregnancy is broken into three trimesters, and the length of each trimester equates to roughly three months.

In the first trimester, morning sickness will occur for about two-thirds of all women and will slowly fade away by the end of those first three months. Within the first trimester, the nipples and areolas of the mother-to-be will darken. This is caused by an increase in hormones. Also, miscarriages are most likely to occur during this trimester.

The second trimester consists of the fourth to sixth months. During this period of time, the mother will feel energized and will begin putting on weight due to the growth of the fetus, as well as the increase in size of the uterus. During the second trimester, movement by the fetus can also be felt. This will usually happen in the fourth month, but most women will not feel movement of the fetus until later on in the pregnancy. During this stage, it is also possible to determine the sex of the baby.

The third trimester consists of the last three months of the pregnancy. During this trimester, the mother will have the most weight gain because the fetus is growing by as much as 28 grams per day. The belly of the mother will also drop from its upright position in the second trimester because the fetus is turning in preparation for the birth. The mother can also feel the movements of the fetus at this point, and the navel can sometimes pop out due to the expansion of her belly. During this trimester, the fetus has the best chance of survival if it is born prematurely.

Choosing a Doctor

One significant task that needs to be taken care of early on is choosing a doctor, or OB/GYN, which is a doctor of obstetrics and gynecology. This can be a difficult task because there are several choices and options to consider. The mother may want a female doctor, or you may want a veteran doctor who has been delivering babies for decades. In contrast, the two of you may want a young doctor who makes use of new technology rather than older methods.

In addition, you may choose a doctor who only tells you what you need to know, while another doctor may do everything that they can to make the two of you feel comfortable throughout the pregnancy. You can try to choose a doctor on the recommendation of your friends, or you can also choose your own family doctor if you are comfortable with that person. Most importantly, you should ensure that the mother is not only comfortable with the doctor, but that she likes him or her, as well.

When you are choosing a doctor, talk to him or her about how he or she feels about various pregnancy and birth concepts. These include opinions on:

- Pain relief
- Birthing positions
- The father's role
- Intervention

Insurance is also going to be an issue you should address, and you should find out the charges for any procedures that are not covered by your insurance, lest you get a bill later on that is much larger than you had anticipated for the birth.

When you and the mother have chosen a doctor, the first visit will consist of the doctor researching both of your medical histories, information about the two of you, and administrating some basic tests. This is an important visit because you want to be impressed by the doctor. You want to have trust in the doctor and know that he or she will be ready when the time comes.

Over the next three months, you will visit the doctor several times, during which you will be able to hear the heartbeat for the first time, as well as let the doctor know of any ailments, symptoms, or problems associated with the first trimester.

Coping With Morning Sickness

One of the biggest myths with pregnancy is that every woman gets morning sickness, and that it lasts the entire pregnancy. The truth is that morning sickness typically only lasts for the first three months, and only about 70 percent of women get it.

For many men, this is the early warning system for pregnancy. When your partner starts to feel sick in the morning and is beating you to the bathroom to throw up, then there may be some big news coming your way very soon. The name itself is a misnomer; "morning sickness" can strike in the morning, afternoon, or the evening.

You may think it is logical to assume that if your partner is throwing up, then she is sick — and if she is sick, then the baby may be sick. Do not worry: The baby is not sick at all, and the morning sickness will disappear around the 17th week of pregnancy.

Doctors have found many causes for morning sickness in women. These causes include:

- An increase in estrogen, which can increase by as much as 100-fold during a pregnancy
- Low blood sugar levels
- The relaxation of muscles in the uterus to prevent early childbirth can cause the relaxation of the stomach and intestines as well, which leads to excess stomach acids
- An increase in the sensitivity to odors
- An increase in bowel movements
- The effort of the body to detoxify so that the health of the fetus can be improved. During the start of a pregnancy, the liver and kidneys will increase their activity, which lends evidence to this theory

There are many tips and tricks that have floated around for hundreds of years on how to deal with morning sickness, but one method that seems to work is eating crackers before getting out of bed. That being said, it does not work for everyone — but it cannot hurt to try. Other remedies that are reported to work include:

- Eating freshly cut lemons
- Keeping the mother from having an empty stomach. A good tip is to have her eat five or six small meals per day, rather than just three large meals
- Eating cabbage
- Eating bananas, rice, toast, and tea
- Drinking water or other liquids 30 to 45 minutes after eating a meal

Changing Feelings

During the first trimester of the pregnancy, you will begin to notice that the mother may begin having changing feelings. In addition, you may also notice that you have changed feelings as well. Many fathers are thrilled and excited when they learn they are going to be a father. Many experience many emotions at once, and while excitement is there, so too is fear.

With the topic of fatherhood suddenly popping up in your head, it is normal to suddenly be afraid. You are venturing into unknown territory. You likely do not know that much about babies and now you are going to be a father to one, who will depend on you completely for the first few years of life.

You should not feel guilty for being afraid of the impending changes in your life. In fact, you should talk with the mother-to-be and discuss your fears and concerns, as well as your ideas and expectations of what will be coming for both of you. You are a team, and it is important you work as a team. Do not feel guilty;

be happy and afraid because that is normal for any man who just found out that they are going to be a father.

To help you understand what kind of feelings will be going through you and your partner during the first three months, here is an easy-to-understand guide:

- First Month
  - > Mother
    - She will be thrilled but slightly frightened at the prospect of being pregnant.
    - She will feel closer to you.
    - She will be slightly apprehensive about the coming pregnancy.
    - There will be some crying and mood swings.
  - > You
    - You will be thrilled but also slightly afraid as well.
    - If you were worried about being sterile, you will feel relief.
    - You will have some irrational fears. Surprisingly, one of the most common fears is the fear of not being the baby's father. A study by Jerrold Lee Shapiro, professor of counseling psychology at Santa Clara University, found that of 200 soon-to-be fathers, 60 percent interviewed expressed this fear. This comes from men's insecurity that they are incapable of creating a life.
- Second Month
  - > Mother
    - She will continue to be excited about the pregnancy.

- She will have trouble keeping her mind on tasks, especially at work.
- She may feel fear that you will not find her as attractive anymore.
- She will experience more mood swings.
- She may also be afraid of an early miscarriage.

> You
- You will be trying to connect with your partner and her pregnancy.
- You will be trying to grasp the concept that your partner is pregnant.
- You will be jumping between excitement and fear.
- You may find your sex drive is also changing, as are your feelings about sex. Sex may be more passionate than before, but it may also diminish because you have a fear of hurting the baby. As will be mentioned later on, there is absolutely no risk of hurting the baby.

- Third Month
  > Mother
  - Hearing the baby's heartbeat will give your partner a sudden realization of what is happening with the pregnancy and the fact that something is growing inside her.
  - She may feel frustrated about her expanding waistline. She may also be excited about it.
  - She will begin to focus more on what is growing inside of her than what is going on outside.
  - She will begin to bond with the unborn baby.

> You
> - You will feel that the pregnancy is actually happening and that there is a heightened sense of reality to the whole situation.
> - You may feel left out as your partner starts focusing more on the baby inside of her than on you.
> - In some cases, you will feel jealousy. This is normal because your partner will be getting more attention from those around you than you will be. They will be talking to her more about the baby and ignoring you more. In many ways, it is like being the first born when a new baby comes into the household. Do not feel guilty about this; it is all part of being a new father.

The First Ultrasound

The ultrasound scan is an important milestone in the first trimester. It is when you get your first glimpse at the small bundle of joy that is going to change your life forever — and for the better.

The ultrasound itself is a sound pressure machine that emits a frequency greater than what humans can hear. The production of the ultrasound penetrates through the skin, where it measures the reflection of what is inside the body. It can reveal details about the womb, which come through as pictures of the fetus through its developing stages.

In no way whatsoever does the ultrasound harm the mother or the baby. In fact, it is a beneficial thing to do because it allows you to see how the baby is developing and to see if there are any problems with the development of the fetus.

The test can be performed at any point past the fifth week of pregnancy. For the doctors and other experts looking at the ultrasound, they can see a great amount of detail, including the sex of the baby during the second trimester, its fingers, toes, and more. For the rest of us, we usually see a jumble of grainy images that may or may not look like something human. The reasons for an ultrasound will vary depending on the trimester that your partner is in.

In the first trimester, the ultrasound is performed to see the number of fetuses in the womb. Also, if there has been any bleeding or the doctor suspects that the pregnancy is taking place outside the uterus, the doctor will administer an ultrasound. In the second trimester, the ultrasound is used to determine the sex of the baby — if you want to know — and to get an accurate estimate on when the baby is going to be due. In the third trimester, the ultrasound is used to determine the position of the baby; to make sure that the placenta is doing what it is supposed to; and to make sure there is enough amniotic fluid to support the baby.

When you and your partner go for your first ultrasound, you should make sure that your partner drinks a lot of water; typically, most doctors require the mother-to-be to drink 32 ounces prior, but the more water she drinks, the better the ultrasound is going to work.

Once you arrive in the room, a radiologist will put gel on your partner's belly. Then, the radiologist will run the ultrasound probe along her belly while staring at the ultrasound screen to see what he or she can find. The doctor should be able to see a great deal on the ultrasound, depending on the trimester, and he or she will explain the visuals to you.

One neat aspect about the ultrasound is that when it is all said and done, the radiologist will often print a photo for you. This is essentially the first photo of your baby. It may be grainy and in black and white, but it is a precious memory that you can keep with you in the baby's scrapbook for years to come.

Hearing the Heartbeat

During the first trimester, probably around the same time that your partner gets her first ultrasound, the doctor will begin looking for the heartbeat. The reason that drinking 32 ounces of water is required before an ultrasound is to inflate the bladder. A full bladder allows the area in the pelvis to be seen much better. If the bladder is empty, it is much harder to see the pelvic area, including the uterus. This is an important point in the pregnancy, especially for you and your partner. When you hear that first heartbeat coming from the abdomen of your partner, the realization that you are going to be a father may hit you full-force. Before this point, the thought of your partner being pregnant was abstract. Other than some mood swings and morning sickness, there was nothing to really trigger your mind into the realization that a new life was on the way. Now, with hearing the heartbeat, your mind can perceive the baby as something tangible and real. This is a major milestone, and for some fathers, it can be a difficult one to handle.

You should be hearing the heartbeat around the second or third month. At first, it will be hard to pick out and can only really be picked out by the ultrasound, but you will be able to hear it, and that moment of hearing the heartbeat can change you forever.

Miscarriage

One of the most difficult parts of the first trimester is the threat of a miscarriage. Although the mother can physically recover from it quite quickly, mentally, it can be a different story.

A miscarriage is the spontaneous end of a pregnancy at a stage during which the fetus cannot survive, typically less than 20 weeks after conception. As mentioned, a miscarriage typically happens in the first trimester. Studies have found that 75 percent of all miscarriages happen in the first trimester. In addition, it is estimated that one of five pregnancies end in a miscarriage and in most cases happen before the woman ever knows she is pregnant.

There have been several causes associated with miscarriages. For miscarriages that happen in the first 13 weeks, half of all of them are due to chromosomal abnormalities. One example of some abnormalities is Wolf-Hirschhorn Syndrome, which often results in mental retardation in the fetus and usually death soon after birth. In fact, any pregnancy with a genetic problem has a 95 percent chance of ending in a miscarriage. Low progesterone levels can also cause problems that lead to a miscarriage.

In the second trimester, 15 percent of all losses are due to a uterine malformation or cervical problems that can lead to a premature birth. Roughly 20 percent of all second trimester miscarriages are caused by a problem with the umbilical cord wrapping around the child's neck or not providing enough nutrients or waste removal, while the rest are due to a problem with the placenta. An example of this is placenta accrete, which is when the placenta is too firmly attached to the uterine wall, making rupture or bleeding much more likely, and delivery impossible.

Symptoms of a miscarriage typically come in the form of bleeding. Any bleeding during pregnancy is often seen as a threatened abortion, which is the medical term for the possibility of a miscarriage. In this case, half of the women who go to the doctor for treatment for the bleeding go on to have a miscarriage. Miscarriages can be detected through an ultrasound, or through hCG (human chorionic gonadotropin) testing. If your partner has a history of miscarriages, it is important to have the doctors monitor her closely and on a regular basis to see if there is a danger of miscarriage.

It is important to remember that a miscarriage does not mean you will never have a baby with your partner; roughly 90 percent of all couples who miscarry go on to have a healthy baby. According to various studies, miscarriages happen because the fetus is defective due to chromosomal abnormalities, or there is a genetic problem in the fetus.

After a miscarriage has happened, it is important to remember that you still have the chance to have a healthy baby in the future. It is understandable to be depressed at the loss of the baby. The psychological aspect of a miscarriage lasts longer than the physical, but it will pass, and you will be able to move on with your life.

If you worry about miscarriages, here are some tips to help you:

- You will have a baby again. Only one out of 200 women have had three or more miscarriages and never delivered a baby.
- Do not listen to others who tell you the horror of a miscarriage and how it affected their lives. People can be inconsiderate or even rude when discussing this type of situation, so do not necessarily listen to them.

- Do not tell anyone about the pregnancy until it has passed the first trimester, and then only tell the people who will offer you emotional support in case something bad were to happen with the pregnancy.
- Get an ultrasound and hear that first heartbeat. It will greatly help you squash the fears of a miscarriage when you hear your baby's heartbeat.
- Support your partner through the miscarriage if it happens. She will need your help and your support, and it is important that you are there for her if a miscarriage happens.

Changing Your Diet

Do you enjoy a glass of wine with your partner in the evenings? Do your meals consist of whatever the local fast food joint has on special? Well, with the upcoming arrival of your new baby, your lifestyle is not the only thing that is going to change for the next nine months; your diet is going to change as well. Gone are the days of junk food, fast food, and raw fish or meat. Your partner needs a certain type of diet that will provide the baby with all the vital nutrients to aid growth in the womb. Because her diet is changing, that means your diet is going to be changing as well. Here is a quick guide to the food that should no longer be in the house for the next nine months:

- **Raw Food:** Any raw food such as sushi, rare steak, and hot dogs is not allowed. They can create some medical problems in the mother and fetus if the food has any sort of bacteria on it that would have been destroyed with cooking.
- **Junk Food:** Potato chips, doughnuts, candy, and any other type of junk foods are out as well. They are high in calories

and can cause problems when you are trying to create a high-protein and high-calcium diet for your partner.

- **Greasy Food:** It is very easy for your partner to have her digestive balance disturbed by greasy foods. Pizza, french fries, and grilled cheese sandwiches are out as a result.
- **Spicy Food:** If you want to create a lot of morning sickness, then this is the way to do it. Stay away from Mexican food during the pregnancy.
- **Smelly Food:** Like spicy food, some strong-smelling foods create morning sickness. Stay away from certain cheeses, peanut butter, and soups like split pea.

You may want to begin eating organic during and after the pregnancy. The reason is that organic food, by law, has no pesticides on it. It is grown in a natural manner, and studies have found that organic food has more vital nutrients and minerals in it than food that is not organic. Fish is generally good for the body, but some fish carry mercury in them. Try to find organic fish from a local fish farm, rather than wild fish that may have mercury and other pollutants in them.

Alcohol is a total no-no for your partner. Countless studies have shown that excessive use of alcohol during a pregnancy can lead to certain birth defects with the baby, called Fetal Alcohol Syndrome. While you can still have alcohol, you should support your partner by not drinking as well. It can be slightly irritating when you want something to drink but are not able to — then, on top of that, watch someone else drink what you cannot.

Any caffeinated products also fall into the category of a no-no for your partner. Caffeine can cause problems in babies if too much of it is drunk. From October 1996 to October 1998, 1,063 women in San Francisco were studied to see how caffeine affected their pregnancy. The study looked at the first 20 weeks of the pregnancies. It found that women who consumed more than two cups of coffee or five cans of soft drinks a day had twice the likelihood of miscarriage than women who did not consume any caffeine. For those women who did not consume any caffeine, the miscarriage rate was 12.5 percent, while women who consumed caffeine had a miscarriage rate of 25.5 percent.

Conclusion

The first trimester of the pregnancy is one of change. From the first to the third month, you not only learn you are going to be a father, but you begin to see the baby for the first time on the ultrasound, you can hear its heartbeat, and you begin to have the realization that your life is going to change forever. You need to find a doctor and help your partner cope with her changing body, her morning sickness, and her new diet needs. In addition, you need to be aware and ready for miscarriage if it were to happen. This trimester is where everything starts, and it can seem rather daunting at first, but you should remember that you are beginning a journey that will bring you more joy than you could have ever thought possible.

In the next chapter, we will look at the second trimester.

CHAPTER 2

The Second Trimester

> "A baby is something you carry inside you for nine months,
> in your arms for three years, and in your heart
> 'til the day you die."
>
> -Mary Mason, author

After the third month, you move into the second trimester, which covers the fourth, fifth, and sixth months of the pregnancy. As you and your partner move into this trimester, the euphoria of realizing you will be parents has begun to wear off, and the thought of the upcoming six months of pregnancy starts to become more real. This trimester brings up many important tasks that you will need to deal with as well. You will probably find out the sex of the baby — if you wish — during this trimester, and you will need to start preparing your bank account for the imminent arrival of the new life in the home. You will have to help your partner deal with her changing body, which will also have an effect on your sex life during this trimester. Furthermore, during this section of pregnancy you get to do fun things like setting up a nursery, and even beginning activities for the baby, like playing music for them.

Getting Your Finances Ready

It is often said that nothing can disrupt your financial planning or carefully collected savings more than a baby can. When a baby comes, there will be many things you will need to buy on a regular basis — often, things you never bought before.

It is a natural process of the pregnancy that both you and your partner will worry about the costs associated with the pregnancy and the baby, and how your finances will deal with the arrival of the baby in a few months.

First of all, once for the last few weeks of the trimester and for several months after the baby's birth, the mother will need to take time off from her job. It is important that she talks to the bosses at her company to find out their policy on maternity leave. Some companies do offer maternity leave, but there are many companies that offer more than others. Your partner will be away from work for a few months, so it is important that at least some money is still coming in during those months from both you and your partner. Maternity leave can help you with your finances, but unfortunately, there are only five countries that do not offer some form of paid parental leave by law, and the United States is one of them.

There are several costs associated with getting the house ready for the baby, but before we talk about that, we are going to go over the costs associated with having the baby and the immediate time afterwards.

Delivery Costs

According to a 2009 study by the consumer health advocacy group Families USA, about 86.7 million Americans did not have health insurance at one point in 2007 and 2008. Without health insurance, a typical delivery will cost between $5,000 and $10,000. If your partner needs a Cesarean section (C-section), then the cost is about an extra $2,000. However, if there is a premature birth, or there are health problems with the baby, costs can run from $10,000 to as much as $200,000 for a baby born 15 weeks early.

Diapers

Diapers are something you are going to need to get used to changing — as well as buying — with a new baby on the way. Typically, a newborn baby will go through eight to 12 diapers per day for the first months of its life. In all, we are talking about 300 to 400 diapers a month. As a result, you need to buy $75 to $125 in diapers each month. If you want to help the environment, you can try buying reusable cloth diapers that need to be washed. It will not only cut down on how much you are throwing into landfills, but it will also cut down on your costs. You just have to be all right with not only changing diapers, but cleaning them, as well.

Childcare

If both your partner and you are going to be working, then you will need to think about childcare or daycare for your baby when they are ready for it. There are many choices: You can have a family member take care of the child, which is often the cheapest method; you can have your child go to a childcare facility; or you can opt to hire a nanny. The costs for this will range from $100 to $800 per week.

The best way to keep costs down is to plan ahead and find out the options for your baby before he or she is even born. Many areas of the country have waiting lists for childcare, and many parents put their own children on it only a few weeks after they find out they are going to have a child.

Food

If you are providing your baby with breast milk, then for the first few months, the costs of food will be low. But if you opt to formula feed, then generally, the costs of this are going to vary but you will typically pay between $100 and $200 per month for formula.

Nursery and Equipment Costs

With a new baby coming, you are going to need to get a room (if you have one available) ready to be a nursery. In addition, you are going to need equipment in your home for the baby to occupy its mind and to help keep it safe. Consumer Reports (**www.consumerreports.org**) is an excellent source for parents-to-be who are buying such products. Here is what you will need to get and the average costs associated with it:

- **Crib:** You are going to need a crib, and the more you pay the better the crib you are going to get. The cost of this can range between $150 and $1,000. Cribs can pose a danger, so follow these tips to make sure you get a crib that is comfortable and safe for your baby:

- No corner posts where the baby can strangle itself by getting its clothes caught on a post.
- Slats and bars should be no more than two inches apart.
- Crib rails should slide up and down easily and lock on the top.

- **Crib mattress:** You should try to get a firmer mattress rather than a softer one. Studies show that a firm mattress can decrease the risk of Sudden Infant Death Syndrome. This will cost between $100 and $150.

- **Bassinet:** If you want the baby to sleep in your room for the first few months, you will need to get a bassinet, which is a cocoon-shaped bed that babies use until they are four months old. This will cost around $100 to $200.

- **Car seat:** If you are going to travel, then you will need to have a car seat. In fact, you cannot even bring your baby home from the hospital without one. You want to get something that is safe, strong, and comfortable for your baby, and this is where you do not want pinch pennies. Typically, a car seat will cost $50 to $200.

- **Changing table:** You can change your baby in a wide variety of places, but having a changing table will make your job easier and safer. Costs for this will range from $100 to $200.

- **Playpen:** A playpen is where your baby can have some fun while you are busy taking care of various tasks in the home. This way, the baby is safe, near you, and occupied. Typically, you can expect to pay between $75 and $150 for this.

- **Stroller:** Having a stroller lets you roll a baby outdoors and indoors with ease, and it keeps you from having to carry them, which can get very difficult the farther you have to walk. A typical stroller will cost you between $100 and $1,000.
- **Baby monitor:** One of the best devices you can have for your peace of mind is a baby monitor. A baby monitor lets you listen to your baby in the nursery so that you can know if the baby is crying and needs anything. One of these will cost between $20 and $100.

Finding Out the Sex

One big decision that parents have to make during the pregnancy is whether or not they want to know the sex of the baby during the pregnancy. Sometimes both parents want to know, while other times, neither does. But some parents — more often women than men — will refer to the baby as "it" before they know the sex, while other parents will choose to give the unborn baby a nickname rather than refer to the baby as "it" when they do not know the gender.

During the second trimester, the doctor will be able to tell you what the gender of your baby is if you want to know. Rather than let yourself be blindsided by this — where you say you would like to know and your partner says she does not — you should make sure you discuss this with each other beforehand.

Many parents do not want to know the sex because they want to be surprised when the big moment comes. For them, that is all part of the miracle of childbirth. However, there are plenty of benefits to finding out the sex of your baby before it is born, including:

- You will know what color to paint the nursery. Generally, boys will have a blue nursery while girls will have a pink nursery. Of course, there is nothing saying you have to stick to that, and a boy with a pink nursery is fine as well. However, knowing the sex of the baby makes planning things like this much easier.
- You will know what clothes to buy for the baby, beyond gender-neutral clothing like jumpers.
- You can choose a gender-specific name before the baby is born. Some parents get around this, however, by simply selecting a potential boy name and a potential girl name.

The most important thing is to talk to your partner about finding out the sex so that you can both agree on it. That way, there will be no discussions down the road about it when the timing may not be right. Also, if you know the sex and your partner does not want to know, make sure you do not unintentionally reveal the knowledge and ruin the surprise for her.

Your Partner's Changing Body

As your partner progresses through the second trimester, she will begin to show the pregnancy more and more. While this is a completely natural process, some women will be bothered by the fact that they are beginning to look larger, especially if they have spent a lot of time working to keep a certain weight and figure.

It is incredibly important that you are supportive of your partner. You want her to know that you think she is attractive, possibly more so because she is carrying your child. Remember to tell your partner that she is beautiful, and keep showing her attention. You can even show more attention so she knows that you still love her — more than ever, just the way she is.

Here are some tips to help your partner be at ease with her changing body and to help strengthen the relationship between the two of you, and with your unborn child.

- Provide her with plenty of back rubs and foot massages. As the baby develops, these gestures will become more and more appreciated.
- Help out around the house.
- Give her hugs whenever you can. Studies show that hugging your partner when she is pregnant will result in the baby being hugged more when it is born.
- Run errands for her so she does not have to go out and deal with the stress of the outside world.
- Tell her that she is beautiful on many occasions, and that she is going to be a great mother.
- Go away for a romantic weekend together.
- Buy her a maternity dress that you think she will look pretty in.
- Keep telling her she looks good, even as she puts on weight.
- Surprise her with breakfast in bed once a week, at least.
- Take some time off work so you can spend time with her at home.
- Call her from work to tell her that you love her.

The Changing Sex Life

One of the biggest changes that comes during the pregnancy is the sex life between you and your partner. Throughout the pregnancy, you will go through high points and low points with your sex life, depending on the trimester and how "in the mood" your partner is after a day of carrying around a child in her body. Sometimes it will be hard for you to gauge a good time for sex and when it is a bad time. Here is a guide for when there may be increased sexual feeling for you or your partner — and when there may be a decreased sexual feeling.

Increased Sexual Desire

- After her morning sickness has passed, both yours and her sex drive may increase.
- You may find her fuller figure and larger breasts more attractive, resulting in an increase in sexual desire in you. Your partner may feel sexier with her ample figure and also have a higher sexual desire.
- During pregnancy, you will most likely grow closer to your partner, and that closeness can result in an increase in sexual desire.
- Pregnancy can cause changes in hormones and an increase in erotic dreams, which will then translate into more sexual desire during waking hours.
- Due to an increase in blood flow in your partner's pelvic area, her orgasms may be more powerful and easier to make happen, which will result in an increased desire on her part for sex.

Decreased Sexual Desire

- Morning sickness and tiredness may result in your partner not wanting to have sex.

- In 25 percent of pregnant women, sex is too awkward and uncomfortable after the first trimester to be something they are interested in.

- She may feel you do not find her attractive, which will result in a lower desire for sex. This is one reason you should make sure to show her you love her on a regular basis, as we discussed earlier in the chapter.

- The worry that the baby will be hurt during sex is extremely common. The truth is that the baby is in an amniotic fluid-filled sac, and unless the doctor says you should not, there is no worry about the baby being hurt during sex.

- Psychologically, both you and your partner may feel more like parents than lovers, and you may feel that parents do not have sex. Obviously this will pass, but many couples may feel this during pregnancy.

- Your partner may find sex painful for a time and will abstain from it.

Prenatal Communication

Throughout the pregnancy, many experts feel it is important for the father to interact with the unborn baby through communication. Studies have found that babies who had parents doing prenatal communication with them were delivered in shorter times and with less likelihood of a C-section. Also, communication with an unborn fetus has been a practice that has been around for at least 1,000 years.

To do prenatal communication, you should not whisper. You will need to speak loudly, or have a set of prenatal speakers on your partner's belly so that the sound reaches the womb. When you do talk to the baby, speak in a higher-pitched, well-enunciated manner, and you should only do this for about an hour a day so that the fetus has enough time to rest. You can mix things up as well: Try reading a story, reciting a poem, or playing some classical music for the baby.

Amazingly, researchers have found that babies who were stimulated prenatally have:

- Above-average IQs, ranging from 125 to 150.
- A lesser likelihood of crying.
- Longer attention spans.
- A better sleep habit.
- A lesser likelihood of developing dyslexia.
- An aptitude for music and creative talents.

Music is especially important to a fetus as they are developing. There are many studies and stories of parents who have played music for their unborn babies. One story relates how an expecting mother played a cello during her pregnancy as she rehearsed for the symphony. After the baby was born, the only music that would calm the baby when it was crying was the same song she rehearsed on the cello during her pregnancy.

While playing Mozart or Bach may not turn your baby into a genius, it is more likely that he or she will have a love of classical music — and soothing music is also good for your partner. One study found that in a group of 236 women, where 116 had soothing music to listen to and 120 did not, the group with the music had reduced stress, anxiety, and depression after only three weeks of taking part in the study.

Setting up a Nursery

One of the biggest tasks during the second to third trimester is setting up the nursery. Often, parents will want to wait to set up the nursery until they know the sex of the baby; that way, they can begin planning the nursery for a boy or a girl. Putting together a nursery takes planning, and it is also important that you give yourself time to get it done before the baby arrives.

Remember, the due date is an approximate date for the baby to arrive, but it by no means guarantees that the baby will be there on that day. The baby could arrive two weeks early or two weeks late. Therefore, once you know the sex of the baby, get down to business and put the nursery together. If you want to wait to find out the sex, you can paint the baby's room in a gender-neutral tone, like yellow or cream.

First, you may feel it is a good idea to have the baby stay in the bedroom with you and your partner. For the first few weeks, this may be a good idea because it will allow you to get to the baby quickly if it is crying at night. However, as time goes on, the need to have your bedroom back may grow, and you might start thinking about getting a nursery for the baby. Therefore, planning a nursery before the baby arrives, even though the baby might stay in the bedroom for the first few weeks, is a logical choice.

There are several items you should put in the nursery:

- A fan in the room will keep the room at a comfortable temperature for the baby, as does a heater.
- You should have a comfortable chair in the room so that night feedings can be done in a comfortable manner, without you or your partner standing around holding the baby. Just do not fall asleep in the chair.
- Music boxes are a good idea as well. The gentle music will help the baby fall asleep, and it will also help relax them so that they do not cry as much.
- A cradle is a good idea because it can help rock the baby to sleep before you put them into the crib. If you decide to paint the crib, make sure you use non-toxic paint in case your baby gnaws on the crib and ingests the paint. A teething rail on the crib can keep your baby from ingesting paint.
- Baby monitors are inexpensive, and they allow you to hear what is going on in the nursery when you are not there. Make sure you get a set.

One factor many parents do not think about is the lighting of the room. When the baby is crying at 3 a.m., you will need to get up, stumble through the hallway, and into the nursery so you can see what is going on. When you get in there, you will naturally turn on the light so you can see the baby. However, for the baby, the sudden blast of light in their eyes is not only frightening, but it is dangerous. Instead, you should get a small night light so that you can see into the room and make your way over to a small lamp that gives off a soft glow.

When you are choosing a color scheme for the baby, try to pick out light, soft colors that are pleasing to the eye, rather than stark colors like bright green or pink. Choosing a semi-gloss or gloss paint makes the room easier to clean, but you may also want to choose a color scheme that will make it easier for you to adjust the room as the child gets older.

Stuffed animals and other accessories are natural for the nursery. You can go with a hodgepodge of items, or you can go with a theme, such as if you want a Winnie the Pooh or a forest theme. Decorating a nursery can be easier if you adapt a theme's appropriate colors and also buy furniture and stuffed animals that reflect the theme.

Conclusion

The second trimester is one of transition. In this trimester, you are moving from the abstract thought of being a father to the realization that the pregnancy and the baby are for real. This is an important step: You go from the excitement of the new pregnancy to planning for the baby that is only a few months away.

The second trimester is also very important in the relationship between you and your partner. She will begin to show at this point, and it is very important that you visibly demonstrate to your partner that you not only find her beautiful, but that you love her more than ever. Your partner's hormones will be in overdrive, and while you may assume she knows you love her still, she may feel differently due to the pregnancy. Show that you love her every chance you get.

Other major steps during this trimester are setting up the nursery, finding out the sex of the baby, and even dealing with a changing sex life between you and your partner.

This is also a formative stage for your unborn child as well. Interactions with the child through prenatal communication and music will help your baby develop. As we mentioned, many studies have found that this type of communication is not only good for the baby, but it is good for you and your partner.

In the next chapter, we will be on the home stretch: the third trimester and the impending birth.

CASE STUDY: ERIC GROUNDS

Eric Grounds is a 31-year-old corporate analyzer. After attending the University of North Texas and studying hospitality management, business and management information systems, he met the love of his life, Mary Lee. They were married on May 19, 2007, and are expecting their first child at the time of print.

What were your thoughts when you found out you were going to be a father?

I was completely thrilled! Mary Lee and I decided that in early March of 2009 we were ready to extend our family. We had heard many stories of trials and tribulations other couples had experienced, so I was trying to keep myself humble. We were on our way out to dinner with some friends, and Mary Lee suggested that we take a pregnancy test just to be sure because she might have a glass of wine. Her hunch was right, and the test came back positive in the first month of trying. We both felt so blessed and excited.

What was the most difficult transition during your partner's pregnancy?

This is a difficult one to answer in that we have not had any real hard transitions. There are the normal transitions, such as prepping for the room and trying to make sure we have all the proper clothes, furniture, and space. But I think for me personally it has come down to realizing that she and I are no longer the first priority. We have something now that is going to take all of our time and resources.

CASE STUDY: ERIC GROUNDS

I am not complaining about that; it is just that when you go from being independent for 31 years to switching all your focus to someone else, it takes time and adjustment. As a father you have to prepare for this mentally throughout the pregnancy. Women have nine months to adjust and adapt to their new physical, mental, and emotional changes. As a father, if you do not prepare for these changes, you are in for quite a surprise on the day of birth. Things that you normally do — such as going out to eat, movies, date night, taking a shower, or even take 10 minutes to yourself — are now extreme challenges. Although it has not taken place yet, I think we are getting ready for the transition.

What changes occurred in the house during your wife's pregnancy?

We had the normal changes that any couple experiences during their first pregnancy. Of course, alcohol, processed meats, and shellfish all went away. There were a few twists that I was not expecting, such as my wife's extreme sense of smell. I could be on the other side of the house with a turkey sandwich and pickle, and she would ask if I was eating a turkey sandwich and a pickle. Amazing!

Do you worry about being a first-time father?

I have worries like any first-time parent. I have the concerns of: "Will I do a good job? Will I be a role model?" I worry about too many things as it is, so I am trying to keep this all in perspective. I am reading and working with my wife on a daily basis on being a first time father. With the Lord, time, and patience, I don't think there is anything we cannot accomplish.

Did you ever think you would be a father?

I had always hoped and dreamed that I would. I never really thought about having kids at all, honestly, until I met Mary Lee. There were other things such as college and establishing a career that I wanted to accomplish first. When we first discussed having a child, I was like many men in that I was concerned something might be wrong with me. I have heard many stories that couples have to go to the ends of the earth to get pregnant. Fortunately, everything went as planned, and we got pregnant the first try.

What sort of things are you doing to prepare for the baby?

That is a very broad question and can simply be answered with "everything." We are prepping mentally, physically, emotionally, and financially. We are prob

CASE STUDY: ERIC GROUNDS

ably going overboard, but I think we would rather be over-prepared than under-prepared. Everything you take for granted, such as your home, will need to be secured and prepped for a baby. Electrical sockets being plugged up and cabinets being secured are just a few of the things that will need to be secured before the baby's arrival.

Are you ready for the experience of being a new father?

Yes, I cannot wait to be a daddy. I know there are going to be ups and downs throughout my experience of being a father, and I will do my best to be the best father possible. It is my own personal responsibility to show the baby the best way to live life and enjoy it to its fullest. As said by Clarence Budington Kelland, "Henry James once defined life as that predicament which precedes death, and certainly nobody owes you a debt of honor or gratitude for getting him into that predicament. But a child does owe his father a debt, if Dad, having gotten him into this peck of trouble, takes off his coat, and buckles down to the job of showing his son or daughter how best to crash through it."

CHAPTER 3

The Third Trimester

> "In the pregnancy process, I have come to realize how much of the burden is on the female partner. She's got a construction zone going on in her belly."
>
> - Al Roker, television broadcaster

Here we are, the last three months. If this were baseball, it would be the final three innings; if it were hockey, it would be third period. This is it, the last few months of the baby being inside your partner's belly. Now the waiting game before the big moment has arrived, and the realization of the impending baby's birth grows ever stronger. There are plenty of things to prepare for during this trimester. You need to constantly be learning how you are going to care for the baby, and you will be attending birthing classes with your partner. You also need to start preparing for the trip to the hospital, what to do when her water breaks, what the

FMLA (Family and Medical Leave Act of 1993) can do for you, and even talking to your work about the potential need to suddenly drop everything and leave.

In addition, you have to learn about false births; begin planning for after the pregnancy with choosing a pediatrician; and determine whether both you and your partner will be going back to work — or if only one of you will.

This is it; the time is almost here, so let us get you prepared.

Birthing Classes

Practice makes perfect, and practicing childbirth birth should make things easier — as it does.

Things have changed greatly since the 1950s. Back in those days, women went to the hospital, gave birth alone in stark rooms, and received general anesthesia for the pain. Then they would wake up later after having given birth, without even knowing what the sex of the baby was. Men on the other hand, got to sit in the waiting room, smoke a cigar (yes, in a hospital), and wait for a nurse to tell them the baby had been born. In fact, in 1965, a man was arrested for trying to "gain unauthorized admission" to the delivery room to see the birth of his second child.

These days, things have changed, and nine out of ten men are in the delivery room with their wives offering support. Prenatal birthing classes have had a lot to do with that. Now, fathers are on hand to help their partner get through the birth through what they learned in birthing classes.

Selecting a birthing class depends on what you are looking for. Some classes teach about natural childbirth and how exercise and good nutrition is more important during the birthing process. Others teach that taking some pain medication during labor is not a sin and should be used to make the whole process easier.

Typically, classes are taught in groups that are open to participant questions. When you ask questions in the doctor's office (before the birth), you may find the answers are quick and hurried because the doctor has plenty of things to do besides answer your questions. Birthing classes do not work like this, which is one reason why they have become so popular, especially for new parents who have not gone through the process yet.

Another great plus of the birthing class is that it provides the opportunity for you and your partner to go out and meet with other couples who are about to have a baby as well. It provides the ability for you both to also learn from what the other couples have gone through, as some will be there even after their first baby has already been born. You will gain the knowledge of childbirth so that you can make the process easier for your partner, and your partner will gain the socialization aspect of meeting other moms. That way, she can know she is not alone in this, while also learning from the experience as well.

Childbirth classes will also help you learn about the various childbirth methods that are out there.

- **Lamaze**: This is the most common type of method used today. Ferdinand Lamaze created it in the 1950s, and it works on the theory that a learned reflex — like pain — can be overcome by focusing on breathing.

- **Bradley**: This method focuses on the education of the parents for the labor and delivery. It tells the woman that she should go with the pain — groaning, screaming, or even yelling to focus it. Roughly 90 percent of the women who use this method choose to have a natural birth.

- **Leboyer**: This method relies on the belief that because delivery rooms are noisy and bright, it can be very stressful for a newborn baby. As a result, Dr. Frederick Leboyer believes in birthing babies in a dim room, where the mother is completely or partly submerged within water. In both cases, the mother's head is, of course, above water.

- **Dick-Read:** Created in the turn of the century by Grantly Dick-Read, it goes on the belief that fear is what creates pain in delivery. When someone is afraid, the body puts blood in the legs to get them moving faster, and takes it away from the face and even the uterus. Less blood in the uterus, according to Dick-Read, results in pain. By conquering the fear of delivery and relaxing, those who use this method then apparently have little pain in delivery.

Childbirth classes will run about five to nine weeks, but there are some that teach everything over the course of one to three days. Typically, you will pay about $100 to $300 for the course. By visiting the maternity ward or talking to your doctor, you should be able to get a list of places that offer childbirth classes.

Preparing for the Hospital Trip

As the big day draws nearer, you will need to start planning for it by figuring out the trip to the hospital and the system you will have in place for when everything starts happening.

Having a good plan for when labor starts is very important. Sometimes, it can be the difference between your baby being born in the hospital or in the back of a taxicab. Months before you go to the delivery room for the big moment, you and your partner should plan out a route to take to the hospital and determine how exactly you should get there. Even when you get to the hospital, you should take the route to the maternity ward so that you can see exactly how to get there. Any little delay can lead to stress, and stress is something that you do not want when your partner is in labor.

There are three ways to get to the hospital (beyond ambulance):

1. **Driving**: This is one that is often used because it is typically the most accessible. When the labor starts, you can hop in the car and be at the hospital shortly. However, there is one big problem with this method, and that is you. When your partner is in labor, you are going to be stressed and nervous. Being stressed and nervous can cause you to overreact or under-react as you are driving. This can lead to accidents, delays, and more. Unless you are cool under pressure, driving yourself may not be the best choice for you.

2. **Walking**: If you live close to the hospital, this is a safe method to take that also allows you to leave quickly, as soon as the water breaks even. That all being said, your partner may not want people seeing her trying to walk to

the hospital, all the while dealing with labor pains. However, walking can help contractions and make them easier to cope with. If you do take this method, bring money and your cell phone. If things do not go as planned you may have to call a cab, or even an ambulance, unless you want your child born outside the local McDonald's.

3. **Getting a ride**: When you get a ride with a taxi, through a friend, or through a relative, you do not have to worry about driving, and you can concentrate on helping your partner. The problem with this method is that if your partner goes into labor at 4 a.m., you may have trouble getting that friend or relative over — or even out of bed. Even if it is during the day, you may have to wait 20 minutes or more for the friend or relative to arrive, and as much as an hour for a cab in most places. Furthermore, your friend or relative may not like the stress of being on call for a few weeks until the baby is born. If you decide to call a cab, then call at least three different cab companies; whoever gets there first gets the fare. It is not the fair thing to do, but unless you want to wait 30 minutes for one cab when another could be there in five minutes, it is what you need to do.

Before you leave for the hospital with your partner, you should ensure that you have the number of the doctor who is delivering the baby so that you can call him/her immediately. Also, ensure you have an extra set of keys for the car, a full tank of gas in the car, or money for a cab. If you have time, check for any closures on the roads or any construction going on along the route to the hospital.

What to Pack

There are several items that you can pack for y|
will make the entire experience at the hospital much calmer and
easier to handle.

- Bring along some of her favorite music to listen to.
- Bring one of her favorite pictures to give her something to focus on during labor.
- Bring along her bathrobe so she does not have to wear whatever the hospital provides.
- Prepare a bottle of water for her that can be reused. She will get thirsty throughout the delivery.
- Slippers or warm socks are good to bring.
- Bring a nursing bra and some sweatpants or maternity clothes to wear.
- Any toiletries she may need, including toothbrush and comb.

As for yourself, you should bring things that will make it easier for you because this can be a stressful experience for you as well.

- Comfortable clothes are very important. You may be sitting in one place for a very long period of time with your partner.
- Bring some magazines so that you can read them or read them to her.
- If you want to have photos of the birth, or at least photos of the newborn baby, then bring a camera.
- Bring snacks so that you do not have to eat hospital food or the food out of vending machines. Note: This is not for your partner, as she should not be eating during

labor. Snacks that are a good idea include granola bars, sandwiches, crackers, and bottled water.

- Bring a list of all the phone numbers of the people you will need to contact with the big news.
- Bring cash (about $100 to $200), credit cards, and your cell phone charger. All three of these can be used in emergencies.

Even as you have prepared everything for your partner and yourself, you should not forget about the other person that will be joining you after you leave the hospital: the baby! Bring these things for the baby:

- Diapers are going to be needed starting day one, so you might as well be prepared.
- Blankets for the baby are also important.
- A sleeper or sleep sac should be brought with you so that the baby can wear it to stay warm. Make sure you wash whatever the baby is going to be wearing, before the baby wears it.

An infant car seat is vital. The hospital will not let you leave the hospital if you do not have one. To save you driving around looking for one while your partner and baby wait at the hospital, go out and get one early at the nearest department store.

Dealing With the Water Breaking

The signal that delivery is about to start is when your partner's water breaks, although this does not happen to all women. Water breaking is when the uterine cocoon ruptures and all the amniotic fluid that was in it spills out. Naturally, this does not wait until your partner is in the bathtub, or when no one is around. It can happen anywhere, even in line at the bank. When this happens, the first stage of labor has begun. Water breaking can be something as little as some of the fluid trickling out, or it can be a full rush of fluid. When this happens, you need to call the maternity ward immediately and let them know that you are on your way. Whatever plans you had beforehand no longer matter; the time has come for labor, and you better get to the hospital as soon as you can. Call your ride, start the car, or begin walking because the magic is about to begin.

Talking to Work

When you are going to be a father, you will need to talk to your work about the possibility of having to leave early when your partner goes into labor. This is going to be one of the most important days of your life, and you do not want to be stuck in a meeting when it happens. As a result, you should talk with your boss and tell them when the due date is and how, for two weeks before and as many as two weeks after the due date, you are going to need to be on call to leave in case your partner goes into labor. If you worry about your boss having a problem with your leaving, you can work out an arrangement so that you make up time after the baby is born for the time you missed taking part in the birth of your child. You could also hope your child is born on the weekend, but you cannot depend on being that lucky.

Family and Medical Leave Act of 1993

We discussed maternity leave earlier, and explained that the United States is only one of five countries in the world with no paid maternity leave laws in place. But there is one law in place that allows your partner to take maternity leave without fear of losing her job. It comes in the form of the Family and Medical Leave Act of 1993, which allows an employee to take unpaid leave due to a health condition or to take care of a new son or daughter. It was one of the first bills signed by former President Bill Clinton in his first term. Under the law, the maternity leave can consist of up to 12 work weeks of unpaid, job-protected leave for various reasons such as:

- "Caring for the birth of a son or daughter or the adoption or placement into foster care of a child.
- Caring for a child, spouse, or parent with a serious health condition.
- For one's own serious health condition.
- Restoration to the same position upon return to work. If the same position is unavailable, the employer must provide the worker with a position that is substantially equal in pay, benefits, and responsibility.
- Protection of employee benefits while on leave. An employee is entitled to reinstatement of all benefits to which the employee was entitled before going on leave.
- Protection of the employee to not have their rights under the Act interfered with or denied by an employer.
- Protection of the employee from retaliation by an employer for exercising rights under the Act."

Thanks to this act, you or your partner are able to take time away from work, albeit unpaid, in order to care for a newborn son or daughter.

Who Goes Back to Work?

One good thing to plan before the baby arrives is to determine who will be going back to work, and who will be staying home with the baby. In the baby's first few years, it is important that a parent is there with it. Naturally, this cannot always be the case, and a child-care provider may be needed. However, if you and your partner are not going to care for the baby yourselves during the day, then someone will need to stay home with the baby.

After the baby has arrived, you will find your entire life has changed, and in many ways, work will not hold the same importance for you. Here are some interesting statistics from recent studies that show how new fathers change in their mentality with work:

- About 75 percent of fathers consider their family to be more important than their work.
- More than half of all fathers want a work schedule that is flexible so they can spend time with their families.
- More than one-third of all fathers are willing to give up more pay so they can spend more time with their families.
- Almost half of all fathers passed up promotions to spend time with their children.
- A full 80 percent of fathers either want to split parenting equally with their partner or be better fathers than their own fathers.

For fathers, it can be difficult to get parental leave from their employer, and if they do, that parental leave is usually unpaid. As a result, many fathers do not get the chance to take advantage of helping the mother with the baby during the first few months. In fact, one state trooper in Maryland was denied parental leave, and he sued for $350,000 and won. This shows that there are still preconceptions out there that fathers do not need parental leave, but mothers do. However, this is beginning to change as time goes on.

Thankfully, there are some options that you can look into if you want to help your partner take care of the child, or if you want to be a stay-at-home father who still brings in money.

First, you can look into sharing your job with someone else. Using the same office and desk, you will alternate in a working schedule so that you are working equally over the course of a month (ten working days each). You can talk with your employer about this and they may go for it, but make sure your health care coverage stays active.

Second, you can become a consultant to your employer. This provides you with flexibility in your schedule, and you get a lot of tax advantages by doing this because you are essentially becoming a small businesses owner. That means you can deduct a wide variety of items.

Third, you can look into telecommuting. This involves working from home by using the phone and Internet so you can do all the office duties you had in the office but from home. This is becoming more popular as gas prices increase and the Internet becomes more adept at providing seamless and constant high-speed connections.

The most important thing you need to do when you are considering the new work situation is look at your finances and see who is bringing in the most money. If your partner is in a vital position in her company and gets paid well for it, then it may make more sense for you to stay home from work, or to become a stay-at-home dad. Talk with your partner and determine what option is going to work best. Perhaps if more money is needed, you can take a job during the week while your partner works weekends. From the standpoint of the baby, it is always best to have at least one parent with him or her at all times to foster a healthy parental relationship.

Another thing to consider is the possibility that you and your partner may not see much of each other if you need to make money; get into the schedule of one parent working days while the other works nights. Your baby will have constant parental care, but your relationship could suffer due to a lack of connection and contact between your partner and yourself.

Choosing a Pediatrician

Before the baby is born, it is a good idea to look for a pediatrician. This is not the same as the OB/GYN who is delivering the baby. You will need to find a doctor who specializes in treating children, rather than delivering them. Since the baby is going to be arriving soon, you should be ready for it with a pediatrician already being lined up. There is a shortage of doctors in some areas of the country, so you may end up having difficulty finding a pediatrician if you wait too long. Try to look for one no later than the third trimester, as you may have to go on a waiting list.

When you are meeting with a prospective pediatrician, there are some questions you should ask them.

1. What insurance plan is the pediatrician part of?

2. How does the pediatrician feel about vaccinations?
    Some pediatricians are not in favor of vaccinations, but they are the minority.

3. How does the pediatrician feel about breastfeeding?
    Some pediatricians will say you need to have your baby breastfed for at least one year, while others will advocate a shorter amount of time.

4. How long are office visits?
    This is a good question to ask because pediatricians are very busy and may not have time for all your questions. If they tell you that they can spare 20 minutes for you each visit, then you may have to determine what questions are best to ask during that period of time.

5. How many doctors are there in the pediatrician's practice?
    You — or in the future, your child — may want to see a pediatrician that is their own gender. You will want to make sure you can get a male or female pediatrician in the practice.

6. If there is an emergency, can you reach them?

7. What are their weekend and night hours?

Some pediatricians are not always on call 24/7, and that could pose a problem if your child is running a fever at 3 a.m. Therefore, this is a good question to ask a prospective pediatrician.

The pediatrician should be visiting you either the day your baby is born, or soon after. At this point, he or she will also be scheduling the first visit for you with your baby at his or her office. From this point on, you will have regular visits, as often as once a month during the first year of the baby's life.

Understanding False Births

During the third trimester, especially the closer you and your partner get to the due date, false births can not only appear, but become an annoying part of the pregnancy. Medically called Braxton-Hicks contractions, the false birth contractions are caused by the body preparing the uterus for the actual birth. These contractions can actually get quite strong, and that can lead your partner to believe that she is going into actual labor.

There are ways that you can determine which is a real birth and which is a false birth.

Real Birth

- Contractions are at regular intervals.
- Contractions get long, closer together, and stronger as time goes on.
- Your partner's water may break.
- There will be pain in the lower back of your partner.

False Birth

- Contractions are not regular.
- Contractions do not change in severity.
- Changing position can cause the contractions to stop completely.
- There is no additional pain in the abdomen.

Taking your partner to the hospital due to a false birth is not something that you should be embarrassed over. With the impending birth and the built-up stress and nervousness that you may be feeling, it is all right to think that the big moment is happening and to rush your partner to the hospital. However, try to check for the signs of a false birth so that you can save you and your partner the headache of going to the hospital, only to be told that the birth is not actually happening.

Conclusion

The third trimester is a very important time. This comprises the last moments before the baby arrives, and it is when your life becomes very hectic with the imminent arrival of the baby. You will be stressed about the big change coming, but excited about it as well. On top of that, you will feel nervous as you wait for that phone call telling you that the baby is coming.

This is also a time where you begin preparing for life after the baby. You start thinking about the pediatrician that will be taking care of your bundle of joy, and you begin planning who is going to work, how you are going to work, and who is going to stay home with the baby or if either of you are going to stay home.

This is the last moment before the big show, and it can be a stressful time, but it can also be a time you will not forget. It is the last few months where it is only you and your partner — at least for the next two decades — so it is also important to enjoy this time as well.

The next big step is the baby's arrival!

CASE STUDY: CAMERON MOORE

Born in Scotland, Cameron Moore moved to Bermuda in 1997, where he met Beverly, a single mother living in Virginia. After chatting for a while and making visits to Bermuda and Virginia to see each other, they were married and moved to settle in Charlotte, N.C. Beverly already had one child, Amber, but they were eagerly anticipating another child in the household. Tragically, Beverly died during labor, leaving Cameron to raise his stepdaughter and new baby.

What were your thoughts when you found out you were going to be a father?

After three miscarriages, when Beverly told me she was pregnant again, it was the usual, "Let's not get too excited and take it a day at a time." The doctors had figured out why Beverly was having trouble keeping her pregnancy going, so there was cause for a little more optimism. I had always wanted to be a dad, and Beverly really wanted to make that happen, even though at age 39, her clock was ticking. I had a great relationship with Amber, then 8, and very early on in the marriage she started calling me 'Dad'.

What was the most difficult transition during your partner's pregnancy?

As the pregnancy progressed, and it looked like everything was going to be OK this time, we relaxed a little and the excitement kicked in. Beverly, having had a baby before, very much knew what to do and what we would need. She liked to be in control of that sort of thing. I painted the baby room and attend the CPR class. I cannot think of any difficult transitions. Beverly knew what she was doing. She was already a stay-at home-mom, so there were not going to be any changes for me regarding work schedule.

What changes occurred in the house during your wife's pregnancy?

Well, we started accumulating baby gear and clothes, and the baby room, which up till then had been a convenient place to store stuff, needed a lot of attention. I had fun decorating that. Other than that, though, we did not have to make too many changes. Now that I have had two kids of my own, I can definitely say it is not essential to have the baby room completely ready in time for the birth — I mean, neither of mine actually spent much time in there 'til they were around 6 months old. I think getting it ready helps satisfy mom's nesting instinct though, so for that reason it is important. She needs to know that everything is ready and in place for the baby's arrival. Looking back, I am now very glad that Beverly had pretty much everything in place for the whole of baby Alex's first year.

CASE STUDY: CAMERON MOORE

What was the first thought to enter your head when the labor started?

I was so excited, I had to tell someone — I called Patti, the administrator at my employer to let her know that Beverly was in labor. I later learned she had sent a company e-mail to everyone to say that baby was on the way. This was around 9:30 a.m. Beverly seemed to be doing fine — she was actually explaining to me what the various monitoring devices did and what to look out for.

After the tragic death of your wife, did you wonder if you were going to be able to manage being a single father?

I did not really think about it that way in the first few days. It was just day-to-day challenges at that point. I had a funeral to organize and also had to inform everyone what had happened. Alex was in the intensive care unit for the first week, which I would not have chosen, but it gave me time to take care some of these things — I knew he was in good hands, so the "What the heck am I going to do now?" question did not arise immediately. When it was becoming clear that Alex would be OK, and it would soon be time to pick him up from the hospital, I started to worry about the future a little. I had an offer from my sister to go back to Scotland and live with them, but that was never an option, as I could not do that to Amber. Losing her mom was terrible, but also losing her new brother and dad whom she loved would be devastating. The hospital wanted me to join Alex for his last night there. They wanted to make sure that I knew how to take care of him by myself. The nurses gave me some basic training and told me to let them know when Alex woke up during the night so they could help with feeding and diapering. When he woke up I just did it myself, and we both went back to sleep. After that, I did not have any doubts that I could do this by myself. My sister would be staying with me for another two weeks, so I knew I could rely on her for advice. When I drove Alex home from the hospital, I remember feeling like there was a hint of sunlight breaking through the clouds.

When the baby was born, were you overwhelmed?

There were definitely a couple of times when I felt overwhelmed. The first was not really anything to do with Alex. While he was in the hospital, I had a steady inflow of visitors, some of whom were staying in the house. Everyone wanted to help, but there were some things I wanted to do myself. I wanted to personally tell some of Beverly's friends what had happened, and I wanted to do some

CASE STUDY: CAMERON MOORE

normal things with Amber. Everyone wanted to do everything for me, but I needed a little normality back to help me make sense of things, so I started losing it a little. Once the funeral was over, things started getting better. I was of course very sad about losing Beverly, but the fact that I had a challenge and big job to do — bringing up a baby — limited my grieving time. It felt like I was on a mission and had to stay focused, and Alex helped me with this. The other time I got overwhelmed was I tried to go back to work when Alex was about 5 weeks old. I had been working on a project and did not want to let down my employer, who had been so supportive. After two or three days of dropping Alex off at a friend's home for day care, going to work, picking him back up again, I broke down: "This is not how I want it to be," I thought.

Describe the first few months of your baby's life and how it affected you.

Once I decided I did not want to go back to work straight away, my employer let me take 12 weeks' leave. I was prepared to leave my job, but once again, my employer supported me. I wanted that time to bond with Alex and let some of his overseas relatives see him. My friends and neighbors were very helpful and supportive and some would look after Alex for a few hours to let me rest or get things done around the house. I did not find it too exhausting though, and soon I began to really enjoy the role of being a single dad. The bond I had with Alex was more like that of a mother and baby. If he heard my voice in a crowded room, he would always look around for me. To this day, as a 7-year-old — even though he is very close to my second wife, Lesley, who he has called "Mom" since age 3 — he still always calls for "Daddy" when he gets hurt or is frightened.

Very early on, my level of respect for single moms greatly increased. Alex was a very easy-going baby though, and for this I realized I was lucky. I often wondered if that was partly by design — He was probably pampered less than some other babies and very much had to adapt his sleeping habits to suit my schedule. He slept through the night from a very early age, and even trips to Europe did not faze him at all. That baby traveled a lot during his first year. Alex was my little buddy; he went everywhere I went and adapted, which he did very well.

What challenges did you face that other fathers did not due to the unfortunate death of your wife?

Well, of course the biggest one was that I was alone. There was no extra pair of hands available in those early months, other than my sister's help for the first

CASE STUDY: CAMERON MOORE

two weeks. This was not so bad during the period when I was not working, but I knew things would be really hard if and when I went back to work. My solution to this was to hire an au pair to live in the house and take care of Alex during the day. My sister had several au pairs from foreign countries when her children were young, and I thought this was the only bearable solution. Alicja came over from Poland, initially for just a year but eventually started living with Alex and I for more than two years. This changed everything, and the feeling of having a life returned shortly after she arrived. I would highly recommend this route to anyone in my situation. Just having someone there who genuinely cared for Alex and was able to lend a hand with housework was a huge relief. Having another adult in the house was a huge benefit for me too. Also, being able to have some "Cameron time," knowing that Alex was safe and happy, was invaluable.

Eventually, this allowed me the freedom to start dating again. The concept of the au pair is that this person should be treated as a family member, which I was happy to do — Alicja was like the kid sister I never had. Alicja is still a good friend of the family, and she decided to settle here herself and is now married and has a career. One last point I wanted to mention: A challenge I did not need to worry about in Alex's first year was the financial one. Although Beverly had been a stay-at-home mom, she had a modest life insurance policy. This was enough to give me some breathing room, and although I would have managed OK, it eliminated a lot of stress, knowing that I had the option not to go back to work for a while.

SECTION 2

Birth to
Six Months

"It sometimes happens, even in the best of families, that a baby is born. This is not necessarily cause for alarm. The important thing is to keep your wits about you and borrow some money."

-Elinor Goulding Smith, author

So, your partner has told you that the moment has arrived. You grab the hospital bag and you run to car enroute to the hospital, hopefully remembering to bring your partner along. You race through the streets, praying that the baby will be born in the hospital and not in the car, and then you hold your partner's hand as she brings a new life into existence.

This is a defining moment in your life. It is a moment you will never forget. You will be there as something you and your partner created emerges into the wild and begins to cry, signaling its arrival. At this moment, you may get an overwhelming feeling of joy, or even pressure, as you realize that this baby is going to depend on you for years to come. You may also realize that at this moment, you are no longer just a man or husband, but a father. Your life will never be the same.

Throughout this section, we will go from the moment your partner tells you to go to the hospital, all the way up to the first six months of your baby's life. The next six months are incredibly important for your baby. They are the formative years for the baby and they are also going to be six months filled with joy, excitement, worry, and a lot of sleepless nights.

The phase of pregnancy has now passed, and it is now time for you and your partner to become parents to a new life. So, let us begin.

CHAPTER 4

The Birth

> "If nature had arranged that husbands and wives should have children alternatively, there would never be more than three in a family."
>
> -Lawrence Housman, English playwright

"Honey, it is time!"

Those four simple words can send your mind and body into overdrive. At this moment, whatever you are doing, you stop it. If you are planning on going to a movie, watching the big game, or going to work, your plans have now changed. The baby will not wait for the game to be over, for the meeting to finish, or for the movie to wrap up. Whether you like it or not, that baby is coming and your first task as a new father is to get your partner to the hospital.

In this chapter, we will go over the entire birth, from being calm while going to the hospital to helping your partner through the entire process. You will also learn about C-sections, labor stages, and even cutting the umbilical cord.

Remaining Calm

A natural reaction when you find out a baby is going to be coming out of your partner is panic. This is a big moment, and it is up to you to get your partner from wherever you are to the hospital so that the process can happen. A few chapters ago, we discussed how you can get to the hospital, and we mentioned how it can be dangerous for you to hop in the car when your mind is racing. It can be hard to concentrate on the road when you are like this.

This is not the only problem with being nervous or having a full panic attack with the birth. The other is that your partner is counting on you to be stable, and if you are panicking or acting extremely nervous, it can actually create problems for your partner because your emotions will be transferred to her, possibly more so due to the labor.

When your partner gives you the news that it is time to go to the hospital, take a breath. A few seconds is not going to make any difference, so acknowledge that it is time to go, and just breathe. You need to remain calm for yourself and for your partner. You want her to be at ease so the birth is easier, and you do not want to be running around in a panic because you cannot remain calm.

On the way to the hospital, you should keep talking to your partner. Tell her that she is doing great, and let her know you are almost to the hospital. If you are driving, then talk with her. If you are getting a ride to the hospital, hold her hand. This will help keep your partner calm.

Throughout the birthing process, stay calm and collected. Talk to your partner in a calm voice and assure her that everything is going great, and she is doing a great job. Tell her that you love her, and keep her mind on something else other than the pain.

There is nothing wrong with being nervous — that is completely natural — but just make sure your partner sees you as a rock that she can rely on through the entire process. In a perfect world, giving birth would be painless and involve staying at the hospital for 20 minutes. In reality, it can be a painful but extraordinary event for your partner, and it can last hours, or even a day or two.

Remain calm, breathe, and keep assuring your partner that they are doing great.

Helping the Mother

If you think the entire process is stressful for yourself, try being your partner. For her, it is 100 times more stressful. You just have to be there for the birth; she is the one who actually has to give birth to the baby. As a result, it is vitally important that you are there to help your partner get through the entire birth as easily as possible. In many ways, just your being there helps immensely.

The Stages of Labor

There are three stages of labor for your partner. The first stage has three phases, and the last stage actually consists of the point after the baby has been born. Here is a guide to the three stages and what is happening with your partner through those stages.

Stage One: Phase One: Early Labor

This is the phase where your partner's water may break. During the first phase, her cervix will begin to open to about five centimeters. During this phase and stage, your partner will become excited over the prospect of finally giving birth but may begin to wonder if this is actually the birth and not a false one. She will be anxious, and she may feel like she does not really want to do anything. This is called the early labor stage because the whole process is just beginning. This stage is the longest part of the labor, and it can last as long as a few days. During this phase, contractions will be about 20 minutes apart and last for half a minute to a full minute. As time goes on, the contractions will get longer and closer together.

Stage One: Phase Two: Active Labor

When this phase begins, your partner's water may have broken, or will be about to break. If her water is going to break, it will be by this stage. She will become uncomfortable, increasingly so as time goes on, and her cervix will dilate to eight centimeters. At this point the excitement has worn off; your partner will become quite impatient about the pain, and she will start to concentrate completely on the contractions. This phase will last about three to four hours and is much more painful and intense than the first phase. Contractions will be about two to three minutes apart at this point.

Stage One: Phase Three: Transition

At this phase, her cervix will be completely dilated, and she will begin to feel the urge to start pushing. Her emotions will be in overdrive at this point, and she may feel confused, frustrated, and even scared. Do not be surprised if she even tells you that she cannot handle anymore, and that she is going home. It is actually a common thing to hear in the delivery room. The last phase of the first stage lasts only a few hours, and contractions at this point will be coming in groups of two to three in a row. The pain will be very intense at this point, and your partner may begin vomiting if the pain becomes too intense for her.

During this stage, you should:

- Tell her that she is doing great and continue to offer her reassurance.
- Try to distract her by talking to her.
- If it is the evening, you can get her to sleep, as this is the earliest part of labor.
- When she is ready to go to the hospital, call the doctor ahead of time and make your way there.
- Help her with her contractions by focusing on one at a time.
- Provide her with ice chips.
- Offer her massages to help alleviate the stress that she is feeling.
- Keep putting a wet cloth on her forehead to wipe away sweat and help her feel cooled down.
- Whatever she needs you to do, do it for her.

Stage Two: Pushing and Birth

When this stage begins, there will be an increase in bloody discharge as the baby begins to move through the birth canal. Your partner will start to feel that she can now finish the job of giving birth, and this is often the phase where she will get her second wind for the final effort of giving birth. This stage only lasts about two hours and is the most intense part of the entire labor process. Contractions will be 60 seconds in length but will be coming farther apart now. As the baby crowns (its head emerges), there will be a surge of pain, but then immediate relief for your partner as the rest of the baby comes through.

During this stage you should:

- Reassure her and comfort her through the entire process.
- Encourage her to push when she can.
- Tell her how great she is doing.
- If there is a mirror, ask her if she wants you to set it up so she can watch the baby being born.
- Do not get in the way of the professionals as they do their job.

Stage Three: After the Birth

After the birth has happened, the placenta in your partner will separate from the uterus and come out within five minutes to an hour. In most cases, neither of you will know that this happened as you are paying attention to the newborn baby. As for your partner's emotions, one of the biggest will be a complete feeling of relief and euphoria at finally being done with the entire process. She will be talkative, hungry, thirsty, and have a strong desire to cuddle with the newborn baby. This stage only lasts half an hour, and contractions will continue until the placenta is out.

During this stage you should:

- Tell her what a great job she did with the birth.
- Place the baby on her stomach for her.
- Tell her to relax and begin to take it easy.
- Let her bond with the baby; do not try to hold the baby unless she lets you.

Once the baby is born, it will receive an APGAR test within the first minute of its birth. This involves the medical staff looking over the baby's condition by looking at the baby's skin color, measuring its reflexes, its activity, and its respiration. After five minutes, the test will be repeated again. Then the baby will be weighed, measured, given an ID bracelet, bathed, diapered, and put into a blanket.

Labor Contingencies

During the labor, there will be a wide variety of contingencies in place in case the labor does not go exactly as planned. These contingencies are not all bad, but it is important to know more about them in case you have to make a decision concerning them.

Pain Medication

Some couples want to have a natural childbirth, but the mother-to-be will sometimes change her mind when the realization of the pain occurs. As the father-to-be, you should not make the decision as to whether or not to administer pain medication. Only your partner should do that because she is the one who is dealing with the pain. If she wants the drugs for the pain, then she should be provided with drugs for the pain. It is important to talk to your doctor long before the birth about pain medication so that you and your partner can both be informed about it and so that the two of you can make an informed decision of whether you will consider pain medication.

Induced Labor

Once you have hit the 40-week mark of the pregnancy, the baby has finished growing and is ready to be born. However, sometimes the baby wants to stay in the womb longer than planned, and when that happens, your partner may want to induce labor. If the baby is a week or more overdue, then the desire to induce labor may become stronger. There are many methods to induce labor.

Forceps

If your partner has been pushing for a while and the cervix is completely dilated, then the doctor may use forceps, which are long tongs that have scoops at the end to help bring the baby out, but this practice has become less common. All these do is gently bring the baby along the birth canal by guiding it. Usually this type of delivery will give the baby some bruises that will disappear in a few days at most.

C-Sections

According to some theories, a Cesarean section is named for Julius Caesar, who was allegedly born by this method. It is used in about 30 percent of all births in the United States. Before, it was primarily used if there was a problem, as in the baby's head being stuck in the birth canal, but today, it is also used as a form of induced labor, or if the mother has a schedule to keep. According to the World Health Organization, C-sections in any country should not exceed 15 percent of all births. There are risks associated with C-sections, including post-operative adhesions, incision hernias, and infections in the wounds. There can also be risk of blood loss and post-spinal headaches. Also, women who have multiple Cesarean sections are more likely to have problems in later pregnancies, according to *Obstetrics and Gynecology*. However, in emergency situations, C-sections can save the life of both the mother and baby. For this reason, it is important to choose to have a vaginal birth rather than a C-section, and if the decision to have a C-section comes up, it should be the doctor who makes the decision because he or she will know whether it is needed.

During a C-section, an incision will be made in your partner's abdomen, and the physician will literally reach in and pull out the baby. This is done when the health of the mother and the baby is at risk. When a Cesarean is done, your partner will have to remain in the hospital for an extra day or two compared with a natural birth. Cesarean sections are safe, with only 20 of 1,000,000 resulting in the death of the baby. That being said, you should still attempt a natural birth instead of a C-section due to the risks associated with the surgery. In the study mentioned above, it was found that the risk of placenta accrete — abnormal attachment of the placenta to the uterine wall that can kill the fetus — increases from .13 percent after two C-sections, 2.13 percent after four C-sections, and 6.74 percent after six C-sections.

There are several reasons why a C-section would be needed:

1. If the mother's pelvis is too small that it cannot allow the baby's head to move through the birth canal.
2. If the labor is a very long one and the mother is exhausted, she may not be able to push the baby out.
3. If the heartbeat of the baby drops at all to dangerous levels.

4. If there is more than one baby coming.

5. If the mother has an outbreak of herpes.

6. If there is a problem with the placenta that can threaten the life of both the mother and the baby.

7. If the baby is coming out feet-first or sideways.

8. If the fetus weighs more than 8 1/2 pounds.

After the C-section, your partner will have a painful incision for several days and will be receiving an IV until her bowels begin to function properly. Hospital staff will also visit your partner on a regular basis, and before leaving the hospital, she will have to have staples removed from the C-section.

Cutting the Umbilical Cord

Throughout the pregnancy, the baby receives oxygen and nutrients from the mother through the umbilical cord, which is made up of arteries and veins. When the baby is born, this 4-foot cord comes with it, and it is at this point the doctor may ask you if you want to cut the cord.

It may come as a shock to you; you may think that because he or she is the doctor, then he or she should be doing these procedures, but it is actually a very safe thing to do, and there is really no wrong way to do it. The doctor will provide you with what you need to cut the umbilical cord, and you simply cut it. Some fathers have described it like cutting a rubber garden hose. If you want to cut the umbilical cord, make sure to talk to the doctor beforehand, as not all doctors offer the father the chance to cut the umbilical cord. The doctor will usually be more than happy to comply.

Conclusion

The birth is one of the most important moments in your life, and it is important that you are not only there physically for your partner, but emotionally as well. Your partner will be looking to you for support as she goes through the labor, and it is important that you not only look calm, but that you reassure her as much as you can. It is surprising just how much that can help when your partner is going through labor.

In addition, by understanding the various parts of the labor process, you can learn how to better help the mother through it. You can also learn about the methods that are available in case the birth does not go as planned so that you are not worrying that something is horribly wrong. Lastly, by understanding the risks of a C-section and when it should and should not be used, it will help you allow the doctor to make the decision, rather than you or your partner.

Now the real journey begins: caring for the baby.

CASE STUDY: RYAN HOLOTA

Living in Canada in Regina, Saskatchewan, Ryan Holota, 33, has been married to his wife for 12 years. A self-described news junkie and car guy, he currently runs several dad blogs to help others deal with the experience of being a new father.

What were your thoughts when you found out you were going to be a father?

My wife and I were married for some time before we decided that it was the right time to have children, so I was completely thrilled when I found out. I really could not have been happier, but I think there was still a part of me that did not believe it at first.

What was the most difficult transition during your partner's pregnancy?

The pregnancy itself was easy for me, but there were these moments when I realized that my life was going to change forever, especially once my wife started to show. They were not negative changes, but it slowly dawned on me that sleeping in on the weekend and doing whatever I wanted were going to be things of the past. It is worth it, though.

What was one of your happiest memories of your wife's pregnancy?

The ultrasounds are amazing. The little pictures they print out are nice, but the actual experience of being in the room and watching the baby move around is hard to describe. I found myself saying, "Hello, baby, I'm your Daddy. I can't wait to meet you." I strongly encourage men to go to the ultrasounds.

What changes occurred in the house during your wife's pregnancy?

There were a lot of changes made to the house itself. Our home office was dismantled to create the nursery, and for some reason, we also thought it would be a good idea to renovate our kitchen. It turns out that this was not a good idea, as the baby came before we finished. It was difficult to find the time to finish it afterward. We spent a lot of time on the nursery. I think this was really important because seeing the room take shape, with a crib and a change table, really brought it home and helped me to prepare mentally.

What was the first thought to enter your head when the labor started?

It was late in the evening, around 11 p.m. I had just gotten home from working out of town and was getting ready to crawl into bed when my wife said that

CASE STUDY: RYAN HOLOTA

her water had broken. She did not have any pain yet, so we called the hospital to find out what to do. They told us that the baby was coming soon and to get to the hospital. I am not sure what my first thought was. It was so sudden, and my wife was not feeling any pain; it was not like in the movies. I guess I thought, "I can't believe this is going to happen tonight." Things got real pretty quick once we got to the hospital, though — eventually, it looks just like it does in the labor videos, which is pretty intense.

What resources did you use to try and learn about being a father?

I started to read "What to Expect When You Are Expecting," but found most of the information in the book was about the biological changes of pregnancy. There was one section specifically for fathers that was good, also some of the general information was interesting. I spent quite a bit of time online researching.

My wife and I also attended parenting classes through the health care system. The classes were interesting, and we learned a lot about the mechanics of being a parent.

What made you decide to start blogging about your fatherhood experience?

I really wanted to be a good dad. I have always thought that one way to be good at something is to think about being good at it, and I thought that if I wrote regular blog posts, I would stay engaged and take on an active parenting role. I hope it has worked out that way.

Describe the first few months of your baby's life and how it affected you.

I am not sure where the phrase "I slept like a baby" came from, because babies do not sleep very well. The first few months were very difficult because you are up every couple of hours. My wife got even less sleep because she was actually up feeding the baby. I did not think my work suffered much, but I was really tired all the time.

It is really important to be as supportive as possible to your wife, because if she is breastfeeding, there are no breaks for her, and it is very overwhelming. I ended up doing a bottle feeding during the night to let her get more than two hours of sleep in a row. You learn a lot about your spouse in that time; I cannot imagine a more stressful situation to put a couple into. It gets easier, though, and over time you look back and say, "Oh, it wasn't that bad." But it really is hard.

CASE STUDY: LEE GUZOFSKI

At the age of 36, Lee Guzofski of Manhattan has been married to his wife, Charity, for seven years. Meeting in New Orleans during Jazz Fest, they are expecting their first child in 2010.

What were your thoughts when you found out you were going to be a father?

Elation. Gobsmacked with realization and responsibility. Essentially a thrill unlike any I have known, sprinkled with abject terror. We had been trying for about two years and in a great sort of full-circle moment, we found out at the New Orleans Jazz and Heritage Festival, which was nine years to the weekend of when we first met back down on the bayou. Hence we have taken to calling our larval offspring "Li'l Gator."

What was the most difficult transition during your partner's pregnancy?

Honestly, we have been sort of already prepared, as we have been trying so long. But the hardest thing so far has just been keeping the blessed news from the prying eyes of our nosy friends. We are both very social and are blessed with a large circle of wonderful — and curious — friends. So when we returned from Jazz Fest, and everyone wanted to get together to hear our stories from New Orleans, they all suspected something was up when we started living like hermits. Other than that, Charity has been great. No odd cravings, and some discomfiture, but nothing crippling or difficult. Again, with full truth, what we thought would be the biggest transition would be curtailing our adventurous, travel-filled, and fun-loving schedule. But we have done that with nary a thought, and it has been easy.

What changes occurred in the house during your wife's pregnancy?

We are still early on, so not very much yet. One of the largest things, though, is going to be making room. We live in a comfortable apartment by Manhattan standards, but one that I imagine will get very small with our blessed addition. Starting my company as I have, I predominantly work from home and have an office, with a ton of books and materials. That will all have to go soon to make room for a crib and the preponderance of items necessitated by Li'l Gator's arrival, due Jan. 6, 2010.

CASE STUDY: LEE GUZOFSKI

Are you nervous about the labor?

About the labor? No, not really at all. Seems to me that Charity has got the hard bit. Now, I in no way ever want to see my wife in pain, but there is a miracle waiting on the other side.

What do you plan to do with the baby when it is born, activity-wise?

Really? I have not thought that far ahead. Particularly in Manhattan, I think that kids get overscheduled and rushed into adulthood. I watched a friend go through pre-school interviews with his 4-year-old son Will. One woman at one school asked, in complete sincerity, "So what are Will's hobbies?"

My friend wanted to reply, "You mean other than stuffing crayons in the VCR? He's four!" But probably replied something like, "Mandarin and astrophysics." My wife and I are abundantly in agreement that children need time to be children and develop their sense of imagination, and embrace their sense of wonder. So as for activities and games, I think we will lean toward creative ones, make believe, and music, plus a lot of time outdoors with physical activities and sports. We have also recently discussed martial arts training.

Have you been trying to increase your knowledge of fatherhood during the pregnancy?

I asked a couple questions to my wife's midwife, who was extremely helpful, but one of them stuck out: "As the male part of this equation — and I am not asking this to 'win points' in any way shape or form, but rather because I genuinely want to know — What can I do to help? Has there been anyone, in all of your years of experience, who ever said, 'You know, it really made a difference when he did (blank)?' Also, conversely, 'What is a sure way to get stabbed, and how can I avoid that?'"

The answers were typical: Pick up around the house, do not tell your partner she looks like she has put on weight, do things without being asked, be emotionally supportive. And I like to think I have done all that and will continue to do so. As for the rest of the stuff, my wife has been doing an incredible job of studying, and she gives me a lot of the info I need to know. So we are both increasing our knowledge, sharing that knowledge, and make a pretty darn good team, if I do say so myself, and I like to think that is the way it should be.

CHAPTER 5

Bringing the
Baby Home

The moment a child is born,
the mother is also born.
She never existed before.
The woman existed, but the mother, never.
A mother is something absolutely new.

-Rajneesh, Indian teacher

Your partner has been released from the hospital, the baby is dressed in its new outfits, and everyone is aching for the chance to come by and see the newborn bundle of joy.

There are many things to consider when you bring the baby home for the first time. You need to deal with crying and feedings, knowing how to share duties with your partner, adjusting your schedules, putting in a car seat if you decided to upgrade models, helping your partner after the birth, changing diapers, and even determining how your baby is going to interact with the pets in the house.

These first few weeks are going to be important for the development of the baby, and it is important that you, the house, and everything in the house is ready for the newborn baby. For the next few years, nearly everything in that house will revolve around the baby.

Your Room or the Nursery?

One decision you will need to make before the baby goes to sleep for the night, or at least a portion of it, is whether the baby will sleep in the bedroom with you and your partner, or in the nursery. Most pediatricians will tell you that you should have the baby sleep alone as soon as possible so that he or she can adapt to being away from you. However, outside the United States and Canada, it is common practice to have the baby sleep in the same bed as the parents. Roughly 80 percent of the world's population does this. The feeling behind this is that the baby needs to be near the parents, hear them, smell them, and sense them. In terms of an evolutionary need, this is actually important to the development of the baby. Most parents will tell you that they had their baby sleep with them for about one month to six months, and there were no problems with the transition to the crib or nursery. There really is no right answer to whether the baby should sleep in the bedroom or in the nursery. It really depends on the parents, but most parents will want the baby close to them early on because they will be very protective and worried about the newborn.

Some parents, especially fathers, worry that they will roll onto the baby and suffocate them while sleeping. The chances of this actually happening are quite low because we have a high sense of where we are and where the baby is while we sleep. Do you roll onto your partner while you sleep? That being said, in an eight-year study by the Federal Consumer Product Safety Commission, out of the total number of infant deaths associated with adult beds, about 23 percent of children under the age of 2 died from a parent rolling onto them while sleeping. The choice is yours on how safe you feel with the baby in the bed, in a crib in the room, or in their own nursery.

Crying and Late Night Feedings

See that look in the eyes of new parents? While you may think it is joy at their newborn, it is most likely an extreme amount of tiredness. One typical law of a newborn baby is that they do not sleep through the night. Crying and 3 a.m. feedings are all part of the territory when you are a new parent.

When the baby starts crying, it usually means that it wants something — usually food or breast milk. The first thing you do when the baby starts crying is to go to the baby immediately. Some feel that this is just teaching them to cry when they want something, but what you are teaching them is that you are there for them and that they are safe in your arms. However, there are other reasons that the baby may be crying:

- If your partner eats something the baby does not like, the baby may cry when he or she is breastfeeding, or afterward. Some babies may not like the taste of cauliflower, and that taste will make its way to the milk that they are feeding on.

- If the baby is crying, it may be a good idea to nurse the baby more often. The baby may want to be closer to its mother, and this can help alleviate that. Several smaller meals that come more frequently are better for the digestive system of the baby.

- Dairy can cause problems for the baby during the first few weeks. Soy milk and cow's milk that your partner may be drinking could be causing stomach distress in your baby.

- By listening to your baby, you will actually be able to figure out which cries mean what. Certain cries will mean that they are tired, that they are hungry, or that they want their diaper changed. Once you learn the cries, you can respond accordingly.

- Countless studies have shown that the more you carry your baby, the less they are going to cry, so try to carry the baby more often.

If you have gone through all these ideas and the baby is still crying, then it may be time for a plan B. Try these tips to see if it helps alleviate the crying at all:

- Not all babies want to be held the same way. Some want to be held out facing away from you, while others want to be held close to you. Try holding the baby so that it lies along your arm, or you can literally have the baby sit in your hand as you cup and hold him or her in place.

- A pacifier can be your best friend in the first few weeks. The baby may just want to suck on something, and it can either be your fingers, their fingers, or a pacifier. Just do not let it become a crutch; otherwise, more crying will result when you take it away.

- The baby may want a bath because they often find warm water soothing. That being said, some babies do not like to have baths and may start crying more.
- A front pack is a device that allows you to carry the baby in front of you without having to stand there holding them. This is a great alternative if you have things you need to do. Before you know it, the baby may be falling asleep in front of you.
- For some babies, going for a walk or drive can actually cause the baby to fall asleep. Some babies will fall asleep in a stroller or car seat without a problem. That being said, some babies will cry until you have taken them back home.
- If the baby's feet are warm, according to some parents, they will cry less. An extra pair of socks may do the job.

When you and your partner are dealing with crying, there are several strategies that the two of you can use.

First, try to have a system in place where you each take turns dealing with the crying. One person dealing with the crying alone can put a strain on your relationship. Essentially, you are taking shifts between the two of you so that at least one of you has a break between crying. This is a very good strategy to implement, and it can go a long way to helping your relationship and dealing with the crying.

Second, sometimes it can be beneficial for babies to just cry themselves out. If the crying goes on for half an hour, you can place baby in the crib to let him or her cry it out. If the baby continues crying for another 15 minutes, then pick him or her back up and try something else. That being said, you should try everything you can before you let your baby cry it out.

Lastly, it is nothing personal. The baby is not crying to make you angry. It is the only way that he or she has to express to you that he or she needs something. So, try to figure out what the baby needs, and do your best to remain calm and collected as your baby cries his or her eyes out.

As for feeding your baby, there are two schools of thought. Your partner can either breastfeed or provide the baby with formula. While formula has become popular among some, you should never underestimate how important breast milk is for the baby.

Here are some reasons why breast milk is so important.

- Breast milk contains the exact amount of nutrients that a newborn needs.
- Breast milk adapts to the baby's needs.
- Breast milk lowers the chances of a baby getting food allergies.
- Babies fed on breast milk are less prone to obesity.
- Babies who are fed on breast milk have a reduced risk of both gastrointestinal disease and respiratory problems.
- Breastfeeding transfers a mother's immunities to the baby.

One of the biggest benefits to breast milk is that it is free. Unlike formula that can cost $1 to $2 a bottle, breast milk costs nothing and is a healthy and natural way for a mother to feed her child. However, formula can be very healthy for a baby and can provide a good balance with breast milk. Formula is fortified with iron and vitamin D and is as close to breast milk as science can get it. In fact, it is believed that formula feeding has led to a decline in anemia in infants.

Adjusting Work Schedules

While the mother may be on maternity leave, it is important that you, as the father, take time away from work to help out your partner with the baby. Taking care of a baby by oneself can be a lot of work, so it is important to talk with your work about adjusting your schedule so that both you and your partner can share the care of the baby.

It is important for the development of the baby within the family, emotionally speaking, that both the mother and father are present throughout parts of the day. The baby needs to recognize you and see you and your partner as his or her protectors, caregivers, and loved ones. If you are constantly away, the baby may not recognize you as a father figure, and that can cause issues down the road — well after the newborn stage.

Ideally, it would be best to talk to your work and bosses before the baby is even born. That way, you can work out a schedule before the baby arrives and have the blessing of work for the new schedule. We talked in the previous section about how you can adjust your work to the baby, and those ideas still apply here. Working part-time, sharing job duties, and telecommuting are all great alternatives so that you not only help out your partner in caring for the baby, but also provide the baby with a father who is there as much as he can be.

Installing a Car Seat

If you drive from the hospital, you have to put a car seat in your vehicle. If you do not have a car seat, hospitals will not let you leave. Hospital staff will also be happy to help you install the car seat correctly if you have never put one in before. You should find a car seat that is going to be the right type for your child. Car seats vary by age and you do not want a car seat that is too large for your newborn, otherwise it may not work as well as one meant specifically for newborns.

The baby's car seat should face the back of the car in the second seat. The car seat should rest at a 45-degree angle, and it should be no more than one inch side-to-side. If you need to adjust the angle of the car seat, then just put something under the seat to get it to the right angle.

Whenever you are installing a car seat, follow the instructions that come with the car seat to the letter. It is very important that the car seat is installed correctly. How the car seat looks is not what matters; what matters is how safe it is.

Your Partner, Her Emotions, and Your Sex Life

The pregnancy is over; the labor has finished. You may think that everything returns to normal with your partner, including your sex life. But this may not be the case.

In terms of how your partner is doing physically, her body will be going through some major changes, which will include:

- She will have a vaginal discharge that will go on for about six weeks, changing from bloody to pink to brown to yellow in color.
- If there was a C-section, she will be very uncomfortable, and the pain will slowly disappear after a few weeks.
- She may be constipated.
- She will have discomfort in her breasts beginning about three days after the birth. This is because her breasts will become full of milk, and when she is breastfeeding, her nipples will be sore as well.
- She will begin to lose weight.
- She will be very tired, especially if she had a long labor. She will need several days of rest to recuperate.
- She will have small contractions for a few days after the birth.
- She may start to experience hair loss on her body due to the hormonal change in her body.

Emotionally, she will feel a wide variety of feelings following the birth, and for several weeks afterward. These emotions include:

- She may be excited, but she may also be depressed at the same time in the days or even weeks following the birth. One name for this is post-partum depression. One reason that depression develops is because your partner may have been very excited about the birth and the baby, and then in one day, it is all over. From that point on, focus shifts from her to the baby, and like the father feeling jealousy during the pregnancy, the mother can feel it now. There is also a large shift in hormones following the delivery. Instead of telling your partner to cheer up, it is a better idea to begin helping her out as much as you possibly can. Before long, she will get out of the post-partum period.

- She may be very relieved that the whole process is finally over.
- She may feel worried about how prepared she is to be a mother and how good of a mother she will be. She will also worry about breastfeeding and whether she will be able to do it. Both of these worries will disappear soon enough.
- She will want to get to know her baby deeply and will spend a lot of time with the baby, which is good.
- She may be impatient to get back to the way she was before the pregnancy and will want to get back out on her feet and do things again.
- She may have a decreased sex drive.

As for the sex with you and your partner following the birth, it may be a few weeks before things get back to normal. After the baby has been delivered, your partner's libido will fall considerably due to the depletion of hormones following the birth. This can result in painful intercourse as well. Most doctors feel that there should be no sex for three to six weeks following the birth of the child.

While this may seem like a long time, with the care and attention you will be giving to the baby — plus taking time for your own work — there may be no time for any sexual activity for at least six weeks anyway. You both may be far too tired.

In one of the most famous studies of post-baby sex, it was found that only 17 percent of new mothers had sex after one month since the birth. By the fourth month, 89 percent of new mothers had engaged in sex with their partner, and by the child's first birthday, 92 percent were again intimate with their partner.

Beyond the physical need for recuperation before there is any sex, there are some psychological issues that may arise now following the birth of your child.

- When you had sex with your partner before the pregnancy, she was the person whom you loved. However, after the birth, you may see her as a mother as well. That can then remind men of their mother, which can lead to problems getting into the mood. Women also have the same problem being a lover to their partner and a mother to their child. In our minds, mothers are not supposed to be sexual, and that comes into play when we become parents ourselves.
- Some fathers have difficulty being sexual with their wives after they see them give birth to a child.
- During the first few weeks of the child's life, you may feel jealousy because your partner is showing more attention to the baby than to you, which can lower your sexual desire.

That all being said, some fathers find the fact that their partners have given birth to be arousing instead of a turn-off. Why? They now have proof, due to the birth of their child, that they are potent. While this may seem odd to us now, it is a natural part of the male psyche.

Changing Diapers

For the first year or two of your child's life, either you or your partner will be changing diapers. There are two types of diapers you can choose from: disposable or reusable diapers. If you are eco-friendly, then you may choose reusable diapers because disposable diapers number in the billions in our landfills each year and last for centuries, while reusable or cloth diapers do not.

There is no going around it: Changing diapers is not a fun job. It stinks, it is messy, and it can be downright gross. But you will have to change diapers regardless, so you might as well get used to the fact that there will be some messes to clean up. Babies do not have a schedule, and they will use their diaper when and where they want. While this may be liberating for them, it is inconvenient to parents. We all wish babies would use their diapers only at home, but the truth is that they use them anywhere, including when you are at a restaurant and have to go and change the baby in the washroom.

Knowing how to change a diaper can take some practice. The main thing is that you do not want the diaper to get loose. This could cause the diaper to come completely off, or become loose enough that the baby can get it off and play with the stuff inside the diaper — and they will.

Here is how you change a diaper in step-by-step form.

1. Make sure you have everything that you need right in front of you. You will need the diaper (of course), wipes, a cover cloth if you have a boy, and diaper rash ointment. You cannot leave the table until the changing is done.

2. Once you have everything, lay the baby on the flat surface with a towel underneath him or her. Remove any clothes that will impede the changing of the diaper.

3. Open up a clean diaper and put it underneath the soiled diaper. Remove the diaper straps, take the front flap off the diaper, and unfold it toward you.

4. Gently grasp the baby's ankles and raise them so that the baby's bottom is off the diaper, while keeping the lower back on it. Remove the diaper and move it so that the baby cannot reach it with its hands or feet.

5. With a wipe, clean the soiled area of the baby. Wipe front to back to reduce the chance of infection.

6. While you are still holding the baby's bottom up, wipe any bits of stool away. This will take about four to six wipes if you have a diaper that has become very messy.

7. Fold the dirty diaper in half while still holding the baby up. Put it into a tight bundle with all the wipes inside.

8. Lower the baby onto the new diaper, bring the flap over, and tape it around the baby's waist. You do not want to make this too tight, but not so loose that it causes leaks.

9. Pick up the baby and put them back into their clothes.

10. Dispose of the dirty diaper into a plastic bag and into the garbage can if it is disposable.

11. Wash your hands and the baby's hands completely.

Do this a few times, and you should have no problem changing the baby with little effort. At first, it can be a bit tricky, as you need to be doing a few things at once, like holding the baby up while cleaning it and putting the diaper into the trash.

However, that is not all you should know about changing babies. Here are some tips to keep in mind:

- If you do not have a changing table, you can just put a towel on a bed, on the floor, or on the counter. Using the bed is safe and comfortable; the counter can be a bit dangerous; and the floor is often the safest because the baby cannot fall off it.

- As your baby gets older, you will be able to start changing him or her while he or she is standing up.

- If you have a boy, then it can be a shooting gallery of urine if you are not careful. This is why you put the cloth over them so that there is no friendly fire while changing the diaper. You can also stand perpendicular to them to avoid being urinated on.

- If the baby moves around a lot while changing them, you can give them a toy that they can use to keep them occupied. Other tips include just talking to them about what you are doing — even if you do not think they understand — singing, and even playing the radio.

- If there is diaper rash, then you should only use zinc-oxide based ointments on the baby to lessen the chances of the diaper rash getting worse. Diaper rash is very uncomfortable for your baby and will result in a lot of crying.

- Newborn babies can be allergic to various wipes, even those that are hypoallergenic. You can try cleaning a rash with cotton wool by just wetting it and getting the excess water out of it by squeezing it. This may help until the baby is older.

- If you want to be environmentally friendly and do not want to buy wipes, you can just use two warm and wet washcloths. The first washcloth will be used to wipe off the baby's bottom, while the second washcloth will be used to wipe it off after the first cloth has become dirty. You should always make sure that each cloth is laundered before you use it.

- Some babies may have a problem with being exposed, so you can put something over their belly like a sheet to keep them from getting agitated.

- Instead of baby powder, you can use cornstarch-based powder. Many parents are now choosing this because baby powder has talc in it, and talc has been linked to lung and female genital cancers.

Interactions Between the Baby and Pets

There are many different interactions that you need to think about with the baby. The interactions with family members, yourself, and those you meet out on the street are important, but so is the first interaction between the baby and the pets that you have in your house. Primarily, you will need to be concerned with the baby interacting with dogs and cats.

Dogs

Dogs are incredibly loyal animals and can often prove to be a protector of the baby. To make the interaction easy, follow these tips before the baby arrives to get the dog ready:

- Dogs learn by association, and if you are kicking the dog out of the bedroom and putting the baby in it, it may see the baby as something negative. Instead, begin having the dog sleep outside the bedroom weeks before the baby arrives.

- Dogs sometimes panic when they first hear a baby crying. To get them adjusted to the sound of a baby crying, play a recording of a baby crying each day so the dog gets accustomed to it before the baby arrives.
- Begin to get the dog used to the baby by using a doll months before the baby arrives. Let the dog see you change, feed, and even put the doll into a crib. It may seem odd, but it works, and it can help eliminate any problems when the dog meets the baby for the first time.
- Ensure your dog is properly trained so that when you tell it to sit, stay, or lie down, it will without a problem.

Once the baby has arrived, do the following to help the dog adjust to the new addition to the family in the house:

- Do not allow the dog to lick the face of the baby. Babies still have weak immune systems, and because dogs lick many places with bacteria, you may not want it going onto your baby's face.
- Do not leave the dog alone with the baby, and always reprimand aggressive behavior.
- When you arrive home from the hospital, have your partner pet the dog while you are holding the baby. The dog will be excited to see your partner and may jump up, so it is important that she greets the dog and you hold the baby.
- Let the dog sniff a piece of clothing that the baby has worn so that it can bond with the baby through scent.

Cats

Cats are not typically quite like dogs in their reactions to a baby, but that does not mean that many of the suggestions that we went through for dogs cannot be used on cats. In fact, you can use many of these tips with cats, with the exception of the ones that involve commands, as cats are not well-known for listening to commands. However, here are a couple of tips that should help you:

- When you put the crib in place, which should be done before the due date, put something on top of the mattress that the cat finds unpleasant to touch. Just put a piece of cardboard with sticky tape on it in the crib, or cover the crib mattress with tinfoil. That way, the cat will not try to take the crib as its own, and there will not be a problem when the baby arrives and begins sleeping in its crib.
- If you do not want the cat jumping in the crib, you can purchase a mesh cover that acts like a dome over the crib; however, you may find the cat sleeping on top of the mesh tent.

Bathing the Baby

Unfortunately, you are years away from being able to tell your child to go have a bath without your supervision. In these first few years, you should be helping your child bathe. First of all, you should never look at this as a chore. It is the opportunity to bond with your child during bath time.

Typically, you are going to bathe your baby every other day; however, if you find that their skin is getting dried out, then you should cut back on the bathing. It is also important that you do not start the bathing until the umbilical cord stump falls off (within a few hours), and after a circumcision has healed if you have a boy (within a week or so). In these cases, just use a damp sponge to wash the baby.

There are a variety of places that you can wash the baby in. Each has its own advantages and disadvantages.

- **On the floor**: Sometimes you can wash the baby on the floor in a small tub. Many parents prefer this method because there is less chance of dropping the baby and hurting him or her. Make sure you have some garbage bags around the area, as both you and the floor will get wet.
- **In a baby tub in the bathtub:** This is like washing the baby on the floor, but you do not have to worry about water getting on the floor.
- **In the bathtub with you:** The baby tub may seem confining to a baby, so the bathtub may be more comfortable for them. You should only use this option when you are comfortable with the bath-time process.
- **In the sink:** Many parents will either use a tub that docks in the sink, or just have the baby wash themselves in the sink. It is a great alternative because the baby is at the right height, keeping you from hurting your back, and you have a regular source of water. You should ensure that the faucet points away from the baby so he or she cannot be hurt by it.

As for the baby procedure, there are certain steps that should be followed:

1. Pour warm water into what the baby will be bathing in. The water should be warm. To ensure it is not too hot, put

your elbow in. If it is too hot for you, then it is too hot for the baby, as well. In the tub, only put in about four inches of water.

2. Remove the baby's clothes, and put it in the tub. You want to ensure the baby does not get too cold. To keep this from happening, put a warm washcloth on the baby's chest and pour warm water over the baby.

3. Wipe the eyes from the bridge of the nose out. Wipe the face, ears, and neck next. Make sure you wash the baby's neck, as it can get quite dirty.

4. Wash the baby's arms, legs, and torso. Pay special attention to places where dirt can hide, like the armpit, leg folds, and belly button.

5. Wash the baby's hair. You should do this last because the baby loses heat through their head and a cold head means a cold baby. Only put a few drops of shampoo on the baby's head. To keep the shampoo out of the baby's eyes, do the following:

   a. Place a washcloth over the baby's eyes and pour water over its head.

   b. Swaddle the baby so only the baby's head sticks out. Hold the baby over the tub with the back of your forearm, and keep its legs tucked into your elbow. Your hand should support the baby's head. Tip the baby's head down so that the water drains away from the eyes.

6. Dry off the baby.

When you are washing the baby's head, you may notice flakes coming off its scalp. While you may begin to panic, do not worry; it is harmless. It is "cradle cap," which is caused by overactive sebaceous glands due to leftover hormones from the mother, and it usually disappears within three months. You can also massage the scalp with mineral oil to get rid of the flakes before that.

If you have ever tried to grab a greased pig, that is kind of how hard it is to hold onto a baby that just got out of the bath. Thankfully, there are two ways to hold onto a baby that you just got out of the tub. The first is to put a clean, cotton sock on your hand so that you can better grip the baby. Make sure you cut a thumbhole as well. The second way is to hold the baby under the armpit. Just lay the baby's head on your forearm so your wrist supports its neck. Then put your fingers and thumb around its forearm. This will keep the baby from slipping in the tub.

As much as we would like to wish it would not, your baby pooping in the bathtub will happen. So, when it happens, it is best that you are prepared for it. Follow these tips to mitigate the accident and get back to washing the baby.

1. Take the baby out, wrap it in a towel, and put it somewhere that is secure where you can watch it.
2. Drain the tub and rinse it with soap and water completely. Scrub and use disinfectant. Do not let fecal matter go down a sink's drain; rather, empty it into the toilet.
3. Refill the tub.
4. Get another towel for the baby and put the baby back in the water.
5. Begin washing the baby again, hopefully without another accident.

Another thing you should be aware of when washing your baby is the diving reflex. There will be an occasion or two when your baby slips in the bathtub and falls under the water for a few seconds. While you will most likely panic, you should not. Babies have an automatic response that prevents them from breathing in water, called the diving reflex. The chances of any harm coming to your baby when it goes under the water for a few seconds are nearly zero. However, this reflex only lasts a few months, and it is not an excuse to be anything but vigilant with your baby in the tub.

Going Back to Work

Generally, you will be the one who goes back to work first because your partner will need time to recover from giving birth. The baby will be bonding with the mother, and the mother may want to stay home with the baby instead of going to work. That all being said, there is nothing saying that you cannot stay home and have your partner go to work. However, for the sake of this section, we will assume you are the one who is going back to work.

Going back to work is not as simple as just going in when the time comes. Your life has changed, and with a baby, what has likely changed the most is your sleep schedule. A disrupted sleep schedule can play havoc with your body and mind, and that can cause problems at work.

The biggest challenge you will face as a new father going into work is exhaustion. You may find yourself reading the same thing over and over in an effort to understand it. This does not mean you are dumber than you were before, but it does mean your mind has suffered from exhaustion, as perhaps have your cognitive abilities. Several studies have actually found that your IQ will lower based on each hour you have lost to sleep. Your memory will be poor, your speech will be sluggish, and you may even be irritable, which is not conducive at a stressful place like work.

You should ensure that your boss knows you have a newborn. Hopefully, he or she will be understanding and cut you some slack, especially if your boss has gone through having a newborn as well. However, you may encounter a boss who does not care and wants you to leave your home life at home.

While you likely cannot nap on the job, unless you work for Google® (which allows napping and even has nap rooms), it is important to fit naps in whenever you can. A NASA study found that pilots who slept an additional 26 minutes per day improved their overall performance by 34 percent. If you need to find time for a nap at work, you can try these tips:

1. During your lunch hour, go to your car and take the time for a nap.
2. If there is a gym in your company's building, then do relaxation exercises there.
3. If you really need a nap, go to the men's room and take a quick nap there. It may not be comfortable, but it works and provides you with a few minutes of shut-eye.

Beyond napping, there are other tips you can implement in your office to keep yourself at full capacity at work, despite a lack of sleep.

- Have a fan that provides a cool breeze. It is important that it varies the speed of the breeze so you do not fall into a pattern that could cause you to fall asleep.
- Caffeine is one of the most common stimulants.
- Keep notes of everything in a planner or calendar so you do not forget anything.
- Chewing gum is a great way to keep awake. Try some gum that has natural stimulants in it like peppermint.
- On the radio, play music that is sharp and sometimes loud to keep you awake. Do not play easy rock or other slow music, as you may feel encouraged to fall asleep.
- Take time to climb stairs each hour so that you can get more oxygen into your blood.
- Eating short, small-sized meals will keep you awake; large meals will cause you to get tired.
- If you really want to wake up, put your feet in cold water.
- Keep pictures of your baby around so that you can remember why you are working so hard, and so you can show others why you cannot keep your eyes open.

Going back to work, it is important to remember that things will eventually settle down, and you will be able to get into a work schedule that will work for you. The most important factor to remember is that you should talk to your bosses and remind everyone that you have a newborn baby, and things are going to be a bit hectic and stressful for you during that time.

Conclusion

Bringing the baby home is a momentous time for you and your partner. This is the time when the baby becomes a part of your home life. This is also the moment when you notice just how much your life is going to change. Your sleeping schedule will be severely disrupted; your partner and you will not have much time alone together for the next while; and you will have to deal with varying sleeping arrangements, putting in car seats, changing diapers, dealing with the possible conflict with your pets, and bathing the baby.

In addition to your home life changing, your work life is also going to change. At work, you will find yourself tired and having trouble paying attention to the tasks at hand.

With all these changes, and some of the headaches, you will also have more of something else in your life when you bring the baby home: joy. When the baby is brought home, you can look forward to the life of your child. From its first steps to graduating college and beyond, bringing the baby home will lead to more happiness to you and your partner than you ever thought possible. You may be tired, but you will be smiling, laughing, and seeing the world in a new way. The baby is new to the world; everything is a wonder, and you will find yourself experiencing that with your baby. You will see the world through their eyes, and you will find it changes your life forever.

Bringing the baby home is only one step in a long journey that began the day your partner told you she was pregnant.

CASE STUDY: PERRY PERKINS

Perry Perkins is a freelance writer, novelist, blogger, and stay-at-home father in the northwest United States who lives with his wife, Victoria, and 2-year-old daughter, Grace. He has written about being a parent for several magazines across the country. He has also had his stories featured in eleven *Chicken Soup for the Soul* books.

Did you ever think you would be a father?

I have wanted to be a father for as long as I can remember. Though we had some discouraging years, we never gave up the hope of being parents.

What were your thoughts when you found out you were going to be a father?

I was ecstatic when, after two failed attempts, I found out that the in vitro had worked, and we were pregnant. I was also a little fearful of being disappointed again, and all of the concerns that come with being an older father. My first thoughts were of thankfulness and great relief.

What was the most difficult transition during your partner's pregnancy?

We were a two-income family, trying to decide who was going to work from home and how we were going to achieve that income was stressful, as we were unwilling to put our daughter in daycare. Vickie was able to take two months off from work and transitioned to a remote-office situation immediately following the birth, then to self-employment about six months later.

What changes occurred in the house during your wife's pregnancy?

There was a lot of stress and some fear over the success of a full-term pregnancy. We had spent our life savings (and sold our house) to afford the in vitro procedure and, coupled with our age, we knew this was probably our last chance to have our own child. Also, we were living in a very small, two-bedroom apartment, overfilled with all the stuff we had in our large, three-bedroom house, so it got a little claustrophobic.

What was the first thought to enter your head when the labor started?

At first, I was very excited. I felt like, "This was it; we had made it to the finish line." Vickie had a difficult labor (22 hours, ending in C-section), and I remember wishing that there was a way I could take on part of the pain she was experiencing and lessen hers.

CASE STUDY: PERRY PERKINS

What made you decide to write about being a father?

Caring and spending time with my daughter Grace takes up so much of my time and gives me so many great experiences and new insights almost daily. As I was writing full-time anyway, it seemed like a waste to not write what I knew. I often think that Grace teaches me a lot more than I teach her.

When the baby was born, were you overwhelmed?

I think we were both so exhausted by the delivery that we did not have time to feel overwhelmed. We had a lot of time to mentally prepare for Gracie's arrival (12 years), so it was mostly just joyful relief.

Describe the first few months of your baby's life and how it affected you.

Grace had some feeding difficulties the first several weeks we were home. She had to be fed every two to three hours, and it took her two hours to finish a feeding. We suffered some serious sleep deprivation that took us almost a year to catch up on. Vickie would feed the baby during that day and then pump at night so I could bottle-feed her. We did have a lot of support through our friends and church, and without them it would have been nearly impossible. Even so, the first six months with our long-awaited baby were very happy ones.

What games did you enjoy playing with your baby in the first two years?

We played a lot of peek-a-boo and tickling. Gracie is a very happy baby, so almost everything we do (except baths) becomes a game. As she approaches two, her favorite thing to do it go for walks outside. We try to focus on physically active games, as we both have a history of obesity in our families and want to remain as healthy and active as possible as Grace gets older.

CHAPTER 6

The Baby's
First Three Months

"All the evidence that we have indicates that it is reasonable to assume in practically every human being, and certainly in almost every newborn baby, that there is an active will toward health, an impulse towards growth, or towards the actualization."

-Abraham Maslow, American psychologist

Some of the most important months in the baby's life will be the first three. During these months, you will find a lot of change happening in your life beyond what we talked about in the previous chapter. During the first three months, you will be introducing the baby to relatives and friends, as well as nurturing the baby's growing mind and dealing with parental roles for you and your partner.

In addition, there is managing stress, figuring out where to take the baby, leaving the house with the baby, and even juggling work and the baby.

These next three months are important. They will be stressful, they will be tough at times, but they will also be some of the happiest months of your entire life.

Adjusting to Life

Finding out that your partner is pregnant means there will be some adjustments in your life. Bringing the baby home means even more adjustments. Raising a child from that point on means big adjustments.

You will be amazed at how much your life has changed since the baby came along. One year ago, if you wanted to go to a movie with your partner, it was a simple matter. However, now you have to not only think about what you are going to do with the baby, but how long you can be gone and what you have to bring with you for the baby. In addition, you have to weigh the pros and cons of taking a baby to a movie theatre. By the time you are done thinking about and organizing everything, you may find that the movie has already started.

The first thing you need to realize is that in this new life, the baby comes first. When the baby is hungry, it is fed. When the baby is tired, it needs to go to sleep, and when the baby is awake, so are you. It takes some adjustment to realize this, but the sooner you do, the better off both you and your partner will be.

You will have to look at everything differently now. When you go out to buy that really nice sword set that you can mount on the wall, you need to think, "Is that a good idea with a baby around?" Every decision you make needs to be thought of in the perspective of a father, rather than a husband. You need to think about how that decision will affect the baby. Making the decision to work late gives you some peace and quiet, but it also takes you away from your baby and puts more pressure on your partner to deal with the baby. Therefore, it is not an easy decision to make like it was before.

Your life has changed, your priorities have changed, and the sooner you can adjust, the better.

Introducing the Baby to Friends and Relatives

Eventually — probably within a few days of the baby arriving at your home — relatives and friends will come calling to see the baby. While they may feel that it is no big deal, for you and your partner, it can be. While those who visit the baby want to shower it with affection, it can be a lot for the baby to handle. As well, you may not want someone, even a close friend or relative, holding your baby because you may worry about them dropping the baby by accident.

However, by introducing the baby to relatives and friends, you are getting a few moments of peace during which you can relax your muscles and take a breather. You can also begin recruiting people to babysit for the baby. However, before the baby is held by anyone else, have your relatives and friends follow these rules:

1. Anyone who wants to hold the baby must wash his or her hands first. The baby's immune system is still building, and if someone has a virus on his or her hand like a cold, it can mean a lot of discomfort for the baby — and a lot of sleepless nights for you.

2. Many people who hold the baby will be so concerned about dropping the baby that they will be very tense. Babies can pick up on this, and that will make them uncomfortable. The more comfortable the baby is, the greater the bond the baby will have with that person. Tell whomever is holding the baby to relax. It is not a greased pig they are holding; it is a baby, and there should be no worry of dropping the baby (even if you *do* secretly worry).

3. If those holding the baby still worry, have them sit on a chair with their arms crossed above their lap. Then, place the baby in the crook of their arm, where it can be safely held while keeping the baby's head up.

Do not be afraid to tell people to wait to come see the baby until your partner has recovered from the birth. Within a week or two, you should be able to have visitors, but remember, those people who are visiting to see the baby need to respect your wishes. If you do not want someone holding the baby, let him or her know in the nicest way possible. They may be offended, but it is your baby, and its safety is the most important factor in your decision.

Nurturing the Baby's Mind

The first few months of the baby's life are incredibly important for the development of their brain. During this time, the baby is receiving vast amounts of information in the brain due to everything that it is experiencing for the first time. During this time, it is vitally important that you work to tone the baby's mind with new stimuli. Helping the baby's mind develop at this point can help raise his or her IQ and give him or her a greater capacity for intelligence. Many studies have shown that the more interaction and the more nurturing games you have at this point, the higher the IQ of your baby.

Here are several tips for what to do and the games to play with your baby to help develop his or her mind:

- Make eye contact on a regular basis with your baby. Their vision is poor in the first few months, but they can recognize faces. Allow them to memorize your face, even if it means staring at it for hours on end.
- Help your baby imitate faces by making faces. By making faces with your baby, you help them develop the social interaction part of the mind.
- Even though the baby cannot talk to you yet, it is important to have conversations with the baby. Language is vitally important in their development, and they will listen to everything you say and pay attention to the patterns of your speech. Their mind will be working to understand you, and that can help strengthen their young mind and give them better linguistic abilities later on in life. When your baby makes noises like cooing, you can praise the baby and give your voice a higher pitch for him or her to respond to.
- When changing babies, use the opportunity to teach about their body parts. Point to their feet and say "feet," point to their arm and say "arm," and point to their elbow and say "elbow." This will help the baby learn about his or her own

body parts, while helping develop the learn-by-association ability.

- If you are playing games with your baby to develop their mental abilities, it is important to use the colors black, white, and red. The reason is that babies can see these colors much better for the first four months of their life. These colors are also mentally stimulating for your baby.

- You can sing a song for your baby as well. When you sing, the baby learns about rhymes and speech pattern. You can also develop their own sense of rhythm, which can give them better musical abilities.

- Be highly attentive to your baby because babies are extremely attached emotionally to their parents. When they are more attached to their parents, they learn better. This builds their emotional intelligence, and that stimulates the limbic area of the brain, which is where feelings come from.

- Do you want your baby to have a great sense of humor in the future? Then laugh with him or her and tickle him or her regularly. You can help stimulate the part of the brain that deals with laughter and humor, and thereby make it stronger.

- Even though your baby cannot even read yet, it is important to read to him or her. You should read books that are meant for that age group, and the books should have large pictures that are brightly colored. Books meant for infants do not have much of a story, but the pattern of the words is meant to stimulate their minds.

- Teach babies about touch. By putting their hand on an ice cube and saying "cold," you help to develop their sensory abilities so that they can respond better to their sense of touch.

- Developing your baby's taste buds is important as well. Teach them about sweet, sour, and salty foods. It is fun for the baby because they learn, and it is fun for you to see them scrunch up their face when they bite a lemon.

- Basic sign language can be taught to babies before they even speak. There are countless videos and books that help teach babies to use simple signs. This is a great way to teach babies to speak to you without words, develop their body language, and greatly increase their communication skills down the road.

- Teaching the baby about self-awareness is vitally important to the development of the brain. Put a mirror in front of the baby and allow him or her to learn about the baby on the other side.

- Teaching a baby cause-and-effect is very easy to do. Simply saying things like, "I am closing the door," and then doing so will work over time.

- The library is a great place to take your baby when they are developing their brains. Libraries have story times and puppet shows meant for babies. The baby will love it, and you will be helping to create a love of libraries in your baby as well.

- Bath time is a perfect opportunity to develop the baby's mind. Showing the baby how to pour water from one cup to another, using soap crayons to make letters on the wall, and creating bubble beards for the baby to observe in the mirror are all great for developing minds.

- Have the baby begin to use finger paints, clay, and mud to better develop the creative parts of his or her mind. It may be messy, but it can help your baby's brain develop.

- One of the best brain-building activities that you can have with babies is by playing and interacting with them and responding to them. Your baby responds to you by making a face with a smile. Watch how they respond to the faces you make, then change the faces to help keep the baby interested. Once the baby is not interested, the process is over; you want to keep them interested as long as possible so they learn more and develop a longer attention span.

- Your baby will respond to various stimuli. If your baby is interested in planes and pays special attention when they see pictures of planes, then take them out to see them. The baby may only be a few months old, but it is a great way to help the learning process by helping them learn about things that interest them.

- There will be times when your baby watches television with you, but even at a few months of age, what they see can influence their young minds. Have the baby watch shows that stimulate them and are meant for them, like "Yo Gabba Gabba!" or "Sesame Street."

- When your baby is watching you do something, tell them what you are doing in detail. Tell them why you are doing it and what exactly you are doing as you go through the motions. The baby may not understand you, but they are responding to your speech. According to speech pathologists, babies can learn the meanings of words by listening to their parents talk in relation to the things that they are doing. They learn by associating the words you say with what you are doing. You hold an apple and say "apple" over and over, and the baby will understand over time that you are holding an apple.

- Going out for walks with your baby can stimulate the sensory part of their brain. By showing them different sights, sounds, and smells, they will begin to develop better senses, and understand them.

- Socialization is an important part of the development of your baby. Having your baby play in groups and in other forms of playtime will help your baby with mental stimulations and increase their social skills.

- Natural curiosity is important to your baby. While it is easier to put them in their playpen and leave them there, it is important that the baby can crawl around and explore the house for them to learn. Just make sure everything is safe and secure.

It is important that you nurture your baby's mind so that they can learn more about the world around them and develop their mind. Games and stimulation go a long way in helping your baby.

Putting the Baby in a New Care-Giving Setting

In the United States, there is typically no paid maternity leave unless you work for a really good company. Even when you are allocated several weeks of unpaid maternity leave, it does not help much when you still have to pay the bills. As a result, it is possible that both you and your partner will need to go back to work a few weeks after the baby has been born. When that happens, it is time to find a care-giving setting for the baby. Several options exist, including daycare, a nanny, or having the baby stay with relatives while you are at work.

In the United States, 1.5 million children are cared for in the home by non-relatives, and someone who lives with the family, like a nanny, cares for an additional 500,000. Many parents choose in-home care because there are many advantages to it. First, they do not have to take the baby to a daycare or worry about the daycare schedule and sick children at the daycare. In addition, the baby will receive one-on-one care and that can help in their development. The caregiver can also keep you up to date on the development of your baby because they will spend so much time with them.

Many parents have trouble choosing in-home care because they worry about the child being left alone with someone else. This is a completely natural worry, but it is important to understand that there are many people who will care for your baby as much as you do. There are three primary ways to find an in-home child care provider:

1. Through childcare agencies. These are great options because they will have references and histories that you can look at to find the perfect person.
2. Word-of-mouth is also a great way to find the right caregiver. Talk to other parents you know and ask them whom they used.
3. You can even put up ads on bulletin boards, or find caregiver ads on bulletin boards.

Once you have chosen a few caregivers to interview, you can bring them over to the house to interview them. You can interview over the phone, but an in-person interview will tell you much more about the person. You should ask the potential caregiver about their experience, why they want the job, and what skills they can bring to it. For example, if you find someone who is trained in infant CPR, then you have someone who can respond if something happens while they are watching your baby. Better to prepare for the worst and hope for the best. You also want to find people who will cuddle and play with the baby.

A great test for those who are being interviewed is to have them change the baby's diaper. While they are changing the diaper, watch what they do. Do they change the diaper as if they are working on an assembly line? No emotion, but they get the job done quickly? Do they change the diaper while they sing and play with the baby? You want someone who knows how to respond to babies and knows how to make them smile.

If you decide on a caregiver, either one who watches the baby at home or actually lives with you, you should hire them and have them start a few days before you go back to work. That way, you can see how they interact with the baby, and you can get the baby used to them while you are there.

However, before you hire anyone, make sure you check references. It is essential you check references and find out why this person left their previous child care job and what kind of child care provider they are.

Here are some questions you should ask:

1. What experience do you have in child care?
2. How old were the children you have cared for?

3. What was your own childhood like?
4. Would you hit or spank a child?
5. Do you know infant CPR?
6. What do you enjoy doing with kids?
7. Do you have a driver's license and daily access to a vehicle?
8. When are you available to work, and how flexible are you in case of a change of plans?
9. Are you fluent in English?

You can also give them "what if" questions so you can find out how they would respond to various situations. For example, "What if the baby began to break the figurines on our shelf?" or "What if the baby threw up in your purse?"

You should also talk to the caregiver about the following:

- How often the telephone can be used for personal reasons
- The responsibilities of the job, including feeding, bathing, diapers, reading, and more
- If he or she is an immigrant, do they have a green card?
- What does he or she expect in terms of payment and vacation time?

Once you hire the caregiver of your choice, get his or her social security number so that you can use it to get a tax deduction for child care on your income tax. Also, if you pay the childcare provider more than $15,000 in one year, you have to deduct for social security taxes.

If you decide to take the baby to a daycare center, then you should keep in mind that just because a place charges a lot of money for care, it does not mean they are better. There are some places that charge nearly nothing because they just love taking care of children.

When you are looking for a daycare center, you should look for the following:

- Find out the level of training that the center's staff has. The more training, the better off your children will be.
- Are the people working there because they love kids, or because they need the job? It makes a big difference in how they treat your baby.
- What is the safety like at the daycare? Is there a fence around the yard? Is access to kitchens restricted? Are windows locked so kids cannot get out of them?
- Is the place clean?
- How many children are there already in the daycare, and how many caregivers are there? States vary in their laws of how many kids there can be for each caregiver.
- What kind of toys do they have at the daycare? Are they good toys? Will your baby be bored?
- What precautions are in place to keep someone from coming into the daycare and stealing a child? We wish it would not happen, but it does.

Child's Perceptions

As the father of your child, you may feel it is the responsibility of the mother to nurture and for you to discipline, or you may feel that those roles are reversed. One of the biggest adjustments for you and your partner will be assessing the parental roles for each other. It is important to assess these roles early in the baby's life so that there are fewer problems down the road. Knowing who is doing what will allow you and your partner to get into a great pattern that will allow the two of you to be the most efficient with raising your baby. Perhaps you are better at changing diapers, while your partner seems to have better luck getting the baby to eat their food. However, when it comes to discipline, or the baby, it is beneficial if both parents share that responsibility.

Perhaps you have a keen interest in educating the baby, while your partner wishes to be the person who spends time with the baby, bonding with them emotionally and taking them out for walks. It is very important that the two of you talk about what your roles will be. If you and your partner are both acting as the disciplinarian, it can work, but if neither of you do, then issues can come up due to a lack of discipline.

As the father, there are several roles you should take on with your child.

- You should always be a tolerant parent with them. By being a tolerant father, your child will develop a strong feeling of protection with you.
- You should ensure you make a point to be a part of your child's life, especially in school. By taking the role as an active participant, your child will have a strong interest in school as a result.
- You should have the role as the disciplinarian. While this should not be exclusively yours, it does help foster respect in you as the father from your child.
- When you are with your partner in front of the child, you should never contradict what he or she says. It is impor-

tant for your baby, even at a very young age, to have a sense of stability and security. Disputes should be handled in private.

In addition to the roles above that we have outlined for you as the father, there are other roles that should be followed by both the parents to ensure that your child has the proper development based on your parental roles.

- Both you and your partner should be caring to the child. The baby will pick up on these cues, and he or she will see how you are feeling.
- Be responsive to your child and what they need. If you find your baby is scared, then do your best to comfort the baby. When the baby is agitated, calm them down.
- As a parent, you should respect your baby's emotions. By doing this, you are teaching the baby to also respect the emotions of others.
- You need to be supportive, and you need to encourage your child. By doing this, you will help your child develop their self-esteem, and the better the self-esteem they have, the better the relationships they will have with other people as well.

Of course, as a parent, there are ways that you can actually have a negative impact on your child's perceptions. These types of roles and attitudes should not be used with your child:

- If you are insensitive to your child, the child will develop a negative personality, which can hurt their self-esteem.

- Being unresponsive as a father is bad as well. If you do not pay attention to the needs of your child — as in responding if they look cold or hot — you can hurt the child's emotional development.
- Hovering over your child, moving too quickly, or being intrusive with your child can develop problem behavior down the road.
- Dominating your child can be a bad thing as well. If you dominate rather than support, the child can develop emotional and self-esteem problems.

It is important as a parent that you respond to your child in the proper manner. The perceptions your child develops toward you that are based on your actions, even in their first three months, can have a large impact on their development down the road. They are formulating their emotional makeup at this time, and that means that what you do now makes a difference.

Always be supportive of your child, even if you do not think they understand, and never treat your child as anything less than you.

Doing this goes a long way in creating a child with a healthy emotional balance, which is just as important as the physical and mental aspects of the child.

Getting Clothes and Dressing the Child

In the first three months of your baby's life, you will be hard-pressed to keep clothes on it that fit. Babies grow about 1.3 inches each month in their first three months. That means the clothes that fit your baby when they were born are four inches too small for them three months later. Beyond getting them clothes, you are also going to actually put the clothes on them as well. That can be more difficult than you may think when the baby is squirming and does not want to put on the clothes that you have carefully picked out for him or her.

When the baby is born, its clothing size will literally be 000. This is as small as you can get for clothing and it is the only thing that will fit your baby. During this stage, do not buy too many clothes because the baby is going to grow out of them too quickly, and you will be left with a bunch of clothes that the baby outgrew before it could wear them all. You will probably get a lot of clothes in the baby shower or as gifts that you can have the baby wear. The great thing about those clothes is that you can hold onto them, and if you have another baby with your partner, you can simply hand those clothes down to the new baby.

The perfect outfit for your baby is literally their pajamas. This outfit, which covers them from head to toe, blends together both comfort and functionality. The baby can sleep in it, move around in it, and use it for a few months at least. This outfit is often called a sleeper. One great thing about the sleeper is that it does not come with a neck hole. Instead, you button up the front of the sleeper when you put the baby in it. Babies do not like to have their heads put through neck holes that are too small, so your baby will be much more comfortable with the sleeper.

Even as the baby grows, you can cut off the feet of the sleeper so that the baby can still wear the sleeper, just with socks on their feet instead.

It is also important to dress your baby based on the temperature. During the winter, if you live in a cold climate, you will need to provide more warmth than what the sleeper can provide on its own. You should not use a blanket, as they are unsafe for young babies. Several babies in recent years have accidently hung themselves with blankets caught in crib railings. Instead, something like a sleep sack will work. This is a blanket without sleeves or a collar that covers your baby securely and safely, while providing the baby with a lot of warmth that they cannot kick away.

In the heat of the sun, you also need to protect your baby. During the first few months of your baby's life, you should keep him or her out of direct sunlight as much as you can. Cover up your baby with loose and long-sleeved clothing. Also ensure that your baby has sunscreen on and a hat before venturing outdoors. When your baby is sleeping in the summer, you should give them something that provides them with some warmth, but not too much. Onesies® are a good bet. They are loose in the crotch and easy to put on. Then your baby has its arms and legs uncovered so that it does not retain too much heat when he or she is sleeping.

When you are dressing your baby, do the following:

1. Reach your fingers through the sleeve of the baby's jumper, sleeper, Onesie®, or shirt, and pull their hands through. This is a lot easier than trying to push the baby's arm through the armhole.
2. For the baby's pants, you should ensure you buy pants that snap on instead of pull on. This makes it much easier for you to put the pants on the baby. When you are changing a baby, you can quickly remove the pants and put them back on without any fuss, which makes things much easier, especially if you are in a bathroom on a changing table.

Another point is to keep from overdressing your baby. Many parents want to bundle up their babies through all seasons, usually out of a worry for the baby getting sick. A good rule of thumb with dressing your baby is to have the baby wear the same layers that you do. If you are wearing a shirt, sweater, and coat, then the baby should. If you are wearing a long sleeve shirt and no jacket, then the baby can as well. When it is cold out, or even mild, having two layers on the baby is a good idea so that you can remove a layer if you find the baby is getting too hot.

Lastly, do not buy shoes. For a baby who is under three months old, this is a complete waste of money. If the baby cannot walk, then the baby does not need shoes. This is just an aesthetic issue and not a functional one. In addition, the baby's bones are growing at a rapid rate, and confining their feet into shoes all day can hurt and damage their developing bones.

Leaving the House

Gone are the days when a quick trip to the store took you 30 seconds to put on your shoes, five minutes to get to the store, and another 30 seconds to take off your shoes when you get back home.

Now with a baby, everything takes 10 times longer. Going out with the baby is a big procedure, but there are ways that you can make it easier for yourself and your partner.

When you are leaving the house, there are two ways that you will be traveling with your baby. The first is walking with a stroller, and the second is driving with the baby in the vehicle.

Walking With the Stroller

There are several types of strollers to choose from when you are looking to purchase one — if you have not already — for walking with your baby.

The first option that you have is a carriage combo. A carriage combo is a traditional baby carriage that can change into a stroller when the baby gets too old for the carriage. Carriages are the perfect type of stroller for babies under three months because babies of that age need to lie flat. This is for head support. With a carriage combo, the baby can see the parent while you walk. However, the carriage combo is often bulky, heavy, and not very maneuverable.

The second option is a stroller combo. This is like a carriage combo, but it weighs about 20 to 25 pounds, which is considerably less than what the carriage combo weighs. They also maneuver well. However, the stroller has a seat instead of a bed for the baby to lie down in, making it useful for babies over the age of three months.

The third option is a car seat carrier. Many parents prefer this option because you can remove the baby from the stroller and put it directly into the car without having to remove the baby from the seat. Obviously, this makes this option much more bulky than other options. While it is bulky, these types of strollers only weigh 20 pounds and can be found for quite cheap.

The fourth option is a lightweight stroller that is sturdy but expensive, and weighs about 15 pounds. Many of these lightweight strollers can fold their seats back so a newborn can use it. Also, they are often great if you live in the city, the reason being that the strollers do not work well on rough terrain. These models do not allow for much in the way of storage, which can be a problem when you are carrying the baby's travel bag.

Driving With the Baby

When you have to go out on errands, or even drive to visit family and show off the newborn with your partner, you will need to take the baby into the vehicle. This can be a bit more complicated than the stroller, but there are ways to make it easier for you.

Here are some tips to make the driving experience with your baby much easier to manage:

- Take a plastic baby-linking chain and string it between the handles above the backseat windows. Then, hang toys from the links so that the baby can play with them. This is a great option because the baby can play with the toys, you can switch out the toys for the baby, and your view is not obstructed.
- You should keep a large box of toys with you so that you can give the baby new toys to play with. It is very important to remember that the baby will drop toys more often than hold them, and that can cause crying. Since you cannot pick up the toys in the backseat as you drive, you should keep a box of toys up front with you.
- Baby's love white noise and soothing sounds like the sound of wind through the open windows. If the baby is tired, you can use these options to help the baby fall asleep.
- Another option is to scan through the radio stations until you find something that the baby likes, which will help quiet him or her down.

- On a towel over the front seat, tape pictures and black and white patterns. The baby will like to look at the pictures, and it will distract them for a large period of time while you drive.
- Another option is to entertain your baby yourself while you drive. The way to do this is a bit complicated at times but it can be accomplished with these supplies:
  - A hand puppet
  - A mirror that clips to the backseat so the baby can see what you are doing, even though the baby is facing the opposite direction
  - A CD of baby songs

Once you have these items, put the puppet on your hand and ensure the baby can see it in their mirror. Talk in a funny voice to the baby, turn on the music, and make the puppet sing the music for the baby. The baby will love it, and it will keep them occupied. Just make sure you keep your eyes on the road. A better alternative is to have the passenger do this while you drive.

- The car seat is something that is vitally important when you are driving with your baby and it is something you cannot do without. If you are going to be driving with your baby, have a car seat. The best course of action is to read consumer reviews of various car seats and find a car seat that can be adjusted for the baby and infant so you do not have to keep buying a new one. You should never have the baby face the front in the car seat; they should always face the back, and you should get some practice with putting the car seat in the vehicle and making it secure before the baby actually arrives and starts using it.

What to Bring

Whether you are going out with the stroller or going for a drive in the car, you are going to need certain items with you. All of these items should be carried in a gear bag that will hold everything. This bag will help you carry everything easily and in an organized manner. As for what you can bring in the bag:

- **Diapers**: Bring several of these. If you think you need five diapers for the trip, bring eight. Always overestimate how many you need.
- **Plastic bags**: These will be used to carry soiled clothes, diapers, and more when you are out traveling.
- **Wipes**: If you are changing diapers, then you need to have the wipes. You can also use the wipes for cleaning a variety of items for the baby and wiping their chin.
- **Changing pad**: If you need to change the baby, you will need to put them on something to do it.
- **Burp cloth**: A burp cloth can be used in case the baby spits up. If you are going to be gone for a while, you do not want your baby smelling bad from spit up.
- **Spare clothes**: You should bring an extra shirt and a complete spare outfit for the baby as well.
- **Toys**: These are very important because they can keep the baby occupied and not crying.
- **Bottles**: Store breast milk in the bottles, and bring them with you. Just because you are away from home does not mean the baby will not get thirsty. When the baby gets thirsty, it will start crying, and that can put a damper in your plans for a quiet outing.

- **Tape**: If the stroller breaks, or you have to fasten a diaper in an emergency, something like duct tape will work great.
- **Pacifiers**: Always bring three or four of these, even if you think the baby will only use one.
- **Camera**: You are going to want to document everything about your baby, including its first trips out into the world. It is even better if your phone comes with a built-in camera.

Where to Go and Where Not to Go

Certain places can stimulate your baby and help them develop mentally, physically, and emotionally. Some of these places can be trips meant just for the baby, even if you do not need anything at them. The older your baby gets, around three months and up, the greater its appreciation for some of the things it sees around it.

- **Supermarket**: There are countless colors, sounds, and textures to dazzle your baby. Let the baby hold different things like chip bags, bread bags, packaged steak, and more. It will help them learn about the world around them and the world of food.
- **Escalators**: Going up and down an escalator with a baby is actually a great idea. Doing this can help the baby increase its sense of perception and object tracking. And typically, everyone on the escalator will want to see the baby. Just do not take a stroller on it.
- **Pet stores**: Babies will love looking at the animals, and it can help the baby learn about the world of animals and maybe even get a first pet.

- **Museums**: Places like art museums are a good idea as well. There are many different types of art that will dazzle your baby's eyes and help them develop the senses.

Other places are not a good fit for the baby and should be avoided. These places include:

- Any place that still allows smoking is completely out of the question. Bingo halls are a good example of this. Even places with a non-smoking section are not safe, as smoke and chemicals can still make their way over to you and that can be harmful to your baby. Try and only go to restaurants that are exclusively non-smoking. With new smoking laws across the United States, these types of restaurants are getting easier to find.
- If you are going to the doctor's office, it may be best to leave your baby at home with family or a nanny. The baby needs to be occupied while you are with the doctor, and there are plenty of sick people at the doctor's office that could possibly infect your own baby.
- The movie theatre can be hard on the baby's eyes to look at the screen in a dark room, and the movies are usually quite loud, and that can be damaging to the baby's ears. In addition, you need to consider the other movie-goers as well. You would not have your cell phone going off in the movie theatre, and you probably should not have your baby crying in there, either. There is also the worry of your baby needing to be changed during the movie, which means you have to leave and come back. All in all, taking your baby to the movie theatre may mean you spend more time dealing with your baby than actually seeing the movie.

- Obviously, bars and any other establishments where adults frequent are out of the question. It is best to have your baby go to a sitter if you and your partner want to go out to the pub or dance club.

There will be times when it can seem more trouble than it is worth to take your baby out with you when you run errands, or when you just want to go for a walk. You have to carry or push the baby, as well as take everything that they may need during the trip. However, even with all those extra things that you need to do, it can be a very rewarding experience to take your baby out into the world. It is rewarding for your baby because they get to experience something completely new, see the outdoors, and have their minds go into overdrive with all the new sights, sounds, and smells.

For you, you get to meet people who will want to see your baby. You get to see what may be old for you through the new eyes of your baby, and you get to show off your baby to everyone you come across. It can be a lot of fun, and you may find it to be so rewarding that you go out every day with your baby.

Walking with your partner and your baby can be a wonderful experience, but you should keep in mind the places that you should avoid. Places you may enjoy may be places your baby does not. While you may want to take your son to the ballgame, it may be best to wait until they are a bit older and can appreciate it more. You may love the loud explosions of the latest action movie, but your baby might not. Keep these things in mind when you are planning on going out to determine if where you are going is where a baby would want to go.

Think like a baby, and you will find the places your baby will enjoy. The more your baby enjoys the experience, the more you will as well.

Managing Stress

Stress comes with having a newborn baby. Many things are going to stress you out, not the least of which is crying. We have talked about how you can manage crying already, but we will go further in this section and show you how you can manage overall stress in your life.

Stress will come from many areas beyond just crying. There will be the stress and worry about if you are going to be a good father. You will stress about leaving the house with the baby, and you will find a greater amount of expectations on your shoulders with the newborn. On top of all of that is the stress on your time and finances because of the newborn. This can cause greater anxiety and potential problems between you and your partner.

Here are some ways that you can manage your own stress:

- Do not be afraid to ask people for help. You may want to go it alone, and there is nothing wrong with that, but your parents and some of your friends may have experience with what you are going through, and they can lend a hand. Just asking for help can go a long way in reducing the amount of stress that you are feeling.
- Whenever you can, try and take some sick days, or even a vacation at home. Spending an afternoon at home rest-

ing, or playing with your new baby, can help immensely in lowering your stress levels.

- Exercising each day and taking part in deep-breathing exercises, yoga, and stretching are all good ways to reduce stress.
- Take time out for a nice quiet walk, especially with your newborn. Going outside and getting fresh air can lower your stress levels and make you feel happier.
- If at all possible — and it will not always be — try to get to bed early. The baby may wake you up in the middle of the night but the more sleep you can get, the better you will feel.

As for your partner, she is probably going through even more stress than you are. Though you have to deal with a crying baby and work, she may be dealing with a crying baby, nursing, changing, work, and more. Here are some tips to help lower your partner's stress level:

- Your partner will be lactating, and that means she needs to get not only enough nutrients for herself, but for her baby as well. Due to the hectic schedule of new moms, meals can get skipped. Hunger leads to feeling tired and worn out, which leads to frustration and stress. So, try to take your partner a hot meal whenever you can. Even a small snack can lift her spirits and lower the amount of stress that she is feeling.
- Your partner is going to be very busy with the newborn baby, and if she has to also clean up after you in the house, it is going to increase her stress level. Instead of having her clean up, how about you clean up? Housework is on the bottom of her list of priorities, so it is probably best

you do it anyway. That way, the house is clean, and your partner will be happy. Even just washing the dishes, doing the laundry, and sweeping the floor can go a long way.

- Take the baby off her hands as much as you can so she can rest. Whenever you have a free moment and want to spend some time with your newborn, ask your partner if she wants to have a nap while you take the baby off her hands. This gives her the chance to get some rest, which is important for reducing stress levels, and it gives you some much-needed bonding time with your baby.

Crying

When your baby is crying, your body goes into a biological mode that is called an alarm reaction. This is important because it tells us something is wrong, and that we need to do something about it. With the increased stress levels comes an increase in blood pressure, circulation, and oxygen levels to the brain. Babies cry at 3 kilohertz, which is the most sensitive sound our ears can hear, and it can be quite aggravating at times; some would even call it a form of torture.

There are six distinct cries you should be aware of. Knowing these types of cries will help you react to them quickly, stop the crying, and reduce your stress level.

- A low-pitched cry that consists of rhythmic moans that grows louder is associated with hunger. A short cry, followed by a pause, then a louder cry, another pause, and a louder cry are also associated with hunger.
- If the baby is making a soft and breathy cry, accompanied by rubbing of the eyes, then the baby is probably tired.

- If the baby is in pain, a high-pitched cry will erupt from the newborn, usually without any sort of warning.
- A pattern of forceful sobs that grow in intensity usually mean the baby is in some sort of discomfort, usually due to a soiled diaper or being too hot or too cold.
- A low-volume whimper that does not have any pattern, and which stops and starts without a pattern, is a cry of boredom from your child.
- If your baby has colic, then it will cry with a high-pitched scream for hours on end. Each scream will be about five seconds long, and followed by a pause so the baby can catch its breath.

Stress comes with the territory of having a newborn. However, no matter how much stress you and your partner may feel, it does not match the joy you will feel with your baby. For every cry that rips at your brain, there are ten smiles from the baby that warm your heart.

Colic

The bane of your existence with a newborn can be colic. Colic is a prolonged series of crying spurts that last for hours, as we mentioned. The period of colic can last for as much as eight weeks, starting and disappearing without warning. Researchers and doctors believe discomfort in the stomach is the cause, and thankfully, colic does not strike every infant, with only about 20 percent being affected. But there are many different ways to alleviate colic for your baby and help you repair your frayed nerves.

The causes of colic have been rumored to be everything from gas to spicy foods eaten by the mother. If you have five children, you can bet at least one of them will be affected by colic, even if none of the other children had it. Typically, it will appear within the first three weeks of the baby's life and disappear before the baby is four months old. Studies have found that bottle-fed babies are more susceptible to colic than breast-fed babies.

When your baby first develops colic, you should talk to your pediatrician to make sure that it is actually colic and not something that is more serious. Typically, the doctor will prescribe anti-gas medication or give you some pointers on how you can deal with it.

One method to deal with colic is the "Popeye method" of holding the baby. Do the following to alleviate colic in your baby using this method:

1. While standing, bend your arm at the elbow and face your palm upward.
2. Sit the baby on the palm of your hand facing you.
3. Lay the baby down on your forearm so that the baby's head is resting on the inside of your elbow.
4. Gently rock the baby back and forth while you stroke its head.

If that does not work, you can use another method that involves the clothes dryer.

1. Put a towel in the dryer and run the dryer until the towel is warm. Put a cold towel in and take out the warm towel and turn the dryer on.

2. Sit on the dryer while it is moving, fold the warm towel on your lap and ensure it is not going to be too hot for the baby.

3. Lay the baby on its belly so that its stomach is resting on top of the towel and its back is facing upwards.

4. Gently stroke its bottom with one hand and its back with the other hand.

5. When the towel has cooled, replace it with the warm towel from the dryer and start the process again by repeating steps three and four.

Colic is never easy, but it is important to remember that it is not fatal to your baby, and it will pass within a few weeks. The best thing to do is power through it and help your baby get through it with as little discomfort as possible.

Baby-Proofing the House

With a new baby, you are going to have to begin to baby-proof the house. Baby-proofing the house means that you are taking the steps to ensure that your baby is safe indoors at all times, as babies do not know not to drink things from under the sink, nor do they know that they should not put items in the light socket.

In Section Three, we will go in more detail in the Identifying Dangers Reference Guide so you can see a list of places and dangers in your home quickly and easily.

There are many things that need to be secured in your house when the baby becomes a permanent resident. The following is a complete list of what you need to secure inside and outside your home.

- Stairs, windows, ponds, pools, and balconies all need to be secured so that your baby cannot fall into or out of any of these areas. Putting up gates helps greatly and can eliminate the problem entirely.

- Fences, railings, and banisters can be dangerous for the baby. Put vertical slats between the bars to prevent the baby from putting its body through the bars.

- Power outlets all need to have plastic plugs put in to prevent your baby from putting anything into the sockets.

- All dangerous chemicals and household chemicals need to be secured in cupboards that the infant cannot open. Astonishingly, a child is poisoned every 30 seconds in North America, with 50 percent of those poisonings happening at home.

- Shelves, drawers, and cupboards all need to be secured to prevent the baby from trying to climb up them. Babies climb as much as they crawl, and the last thing you want is your baby falling and hitting its head.

- Anything sticking out or dangling within your baby's reach is something that they will grab onto, without a doubt. Therefore, you need to make sure no handles are sticking out from the top of the stove and no dangling cords are hanging from anywhere. That way, you can keep your baby from trying to grab onto something that they should not be.

- Plastic bags can never lie around for any reason. Babies can get their heads caught in plastic bags.

- If it is small enough to put in their mouth, a baby will put whatever it finds in its mouth. This is extremely dangerous because it can mean the baby may choke to death on whatever they put in their mouth.

A good test to find out what is and what is not dangerous for your baby is to pretend you are a baby. You can do this by getting on your hands and knees and crawling around the house, making notes on everything that could possibly be dangerous to your child.

Since your baby's safety is vitally important to you, let us go through the house and find areas where the baby could get hurt beyond what we have talked about, and offer a remedy to keep the baby from hurting him or herself.

Living Room

The living room is where your baby will spend a lot of its time, but it is also a location where there are many dangers for your baby. Baby-proofing the living room is incredibly important. This is where your baby will be crawling, playing, and in many cases, eating.

Here are the various places and items around in the living room that your baby can be hurt:

- **Fireplace:** Be sure to install a screen to keep the baby from crawling into the fireplace.
- **Fire tools:** Place these out of reach to prevent the baby from hitting them and causing them to fall on him or her.
- **Coffee table:** A baby could fall and hit its head along the sharp edges. Put rubber protectors on the edges.
- **Potted plant:** Unless you want your baby eating dirt, you should put some sort of netting over the dirt in the potted plant.
- **Plants:** Some plants can be poisonous to a child who eats too much of it. Research what plants are poisonous and keep all plants out of reach.

- **Stereo:** You may think that the stereo is not something you have to worry about, but children can be very curious and they may pull the plastic knobs off the stereo. If they do this, they may put them in their mouth and choke. Install a plastic shield over the electronics.

- **Glass doors:** Many homes have glass patio doors, but these can be dangerous as well. The baby could walk into them face first and hurt themselves. It is a good idea to put decals on the doors to prevent this from happening.

- **Curtain cords:** Curtain cords are incredibly dangerous for babies. Each year, a number of babies accidentally hang themselves on the drape cords. You should wrap these up so they are out of the reach of the baby.

- **Lamps:** Standing lamps can easily be knocked over by a baby, especially one who is just learning to walk. Secure these so they cannot fall over.

You may be thinking that your entire house is a death trap now, but do not worry. By implementing these safety measures, you can ensure that your baby does not hurt itself and that you have a safe house for your newborn to live in.

Kitchen

If the living room can be a dangerous place for a baby, then the kitchen can be downright foolhardy to have the baby in. There are many dangerous items in the kitchen for the baby, but that does not mean you should keep the baby out of the kitchen. Implementing some baby-proofing techniques in there can make it safe for your baby.

- **Hot beverages:** Putting a hot beverage on the counter or table may seem all right, but a baby that is beginning to stand can pull that off the counter or table and splash it on themselves. Move these out of their reach.

- **Stovetop:** A burner can be a tempting thing to touch but a very painful experience if the baby does. To prevent this from happening, turn the burner in the back on, rather than the burner in the front.

- **Stove door:** The baby can pull open the stove door and get a big blast of heat in their face. To prevent this from happening, install a safety latch on the door so the baby cannot open it, but you still can.

- **Under the sink:** There is a plethora of harmful items under the sink that the baby can get its hands on. Install a lock on the cabinet under the sink and any other cabinet where there are cleaning products or other toxic items stored.

- **Fridge magnets:** If there are magnets on the fridge low enough for the baby to grab, then they are low enough for the baby to put in its mouth and choke. Put these out of the baby's reach.

- **Phone cord:** If you have a phone on the wall in the kitchen, you may have a phone cord hanging down. This can be dangerous for the baby if he or she gets her head caught in the cord and accidently tangles themselves. Put in a cord wrap that is out of the baby's reach to prevent this from happening. Thankfully, most phones today are cordless.

- **Trash:** The garbage is full of interesting smells and textures for the baby to discover. Most of these are things you do not want your baby to discover or eat, but they will if you do not put a lock on the garbage to prevent the baby from eating out of it.

- **Tablecloths:** These may make your kitchen look good, but can easily be pulled off the table by the baby, bringing whatever is on the tablecloth down onto them. Use placemats instead of tablecloths as a result.
- **Dishwasher:** If you have detergent in the dishwasher, there is a chance your baby may figure out how to open the dishwasher to get at it. Put in a safety latch like the one you will have on the stove to prevent this from happening.
- **The kitchen:** The kitchen is difficult to baby-proof completely so it may be better just to keep the baby out of it altogether. Install a gate to keep the baby on the safe side of the door, rather than in the kitchen.

Bathroom

The bathroom is a place where the baby gets its baths and maybe watches you get ready for work. But it can be dangerous for the baby with the many things in the bathroom that need to be secured.

- **Toilet:** While it may seem like it cannot happen, there is a chance your baby could fall headfirst into the toilet bowl. For this reason, you should install a lid lock on the toilet so that your baby cannot open the lid and fall into the bowl.
- **Sink cabinet:** Just like the cabinet under the kitchen sink, the cabinet under the bathroom sink often holds harmful cleaning chemicals. You should install a lock on the cabinet so your baby cannot open the sink's cabinet to get at those chemicals.
- **Toothpaste:** Toothpaste, when eaten in large quantities, can be poisonous to small children. As a result, you should

keep the toothpaste out of reach of your child to ensure they do not ingest any of it.

- **Cords:** Hair dryers, shavers, and other appliance cords can cause a child to get tangled in them. Place these items out of reach so that this does not happen.

- **Bathtub:** While the bathtub is for bath time, it can be dangerous for your baby if they were to climb into the bathtub and slip. For this reason, you should install a no-slip bath rug outside the tub, and a rubber bath mat inside the bathtub. That way, they will not slip when they are in the bathroom.

- **Faucet:** The bathroom faucet, usually the one in the bathtub, is hard and dangerous if the baby was to fall and hit its head on it. Install a faucet shield on the faucet to keep this from happening. Moreover, there is the chance that your baby may turn the hot water faucet and release scalding hot water onto themselves. To keep this from happening, install a scald guard.

- **Shampoo:** Babies may try to eat the shampoo, which can be poisonous like toothpaste, so keep this out of their reach.

- **Razors:** Razors sitting in the tub can be highly dangerous because they are tempting targets for the baby. The baby may grab the razor and cut themselves, or even try and eat the razor, thereby causing even worse damage. Put these out of their reach.

Just like the kitchen, you can install a hook-and-eye latch high up on the door of the bathroom so that the baby cannot get in there unless you are in there with him or her.

Home Office

If you work from home, or just have a den that you use as a home office when you are not at work, then you need to work to secure that place as well.

- **Monitors:** These days, monitors are thin and light, making them easy for a baby to tip over if they got up onto your desk (it can happen). Bolt the monitor down so that they cannot pull it down on themselves.
- **Cords:** Put all cords through a tube so that they cannot be chewed on by the baby and cannot get wrapped around the baby's neck, either.
- **Shelves:** All shelves should be anchored to the wall to prevent them from tipping over if the baby tries to climb on them. You should do the same with CD and DVD racks as well.
- **Trash can:** You throw a lot of stuff out in your home office, including things with staples in them and paper clips. A baby can grab those items and begin chewing on them, possibly swallowing them. To keep this from happening, either put the trash can out of their reach, or install a lock on it so they cannot open it.

Toys

The toys you buy for your baby are supposed to be safe, but toy designers do not always think like a baby, and that can lead to baby toys that are not the best present for your child. Before you hand a toy to your baby, you should do the following:

- Ensure that there is no way any pieces from the toy will break off. If you cannot break it off, then there is no way that the baby is going to break it off. Ensure that the toy is quite sturdy.

- Stuffed-animal eyes can be chewed off and swallowed, so examine stuffed toys and make sure this cannot happen.
- You should make sure that the baby cannot swallow the toy. A great way to test this is to use a toilet paper tube. If you can put a toy through the tube, then it can be swallowed by a baby and possibly choke them.

Other Safety Tips

In your home, there are several other things you can do to make it safe. These are things that are not specific to a certain area. By implementing these safety tips, you are making your home safe and ensuring that your baby will grow up in an environment where they do not have to worry about the various dangers in the house.

- **Find out if your home has lead paint in it.** If it does, remove it and put in new paint. Babies can rip off paint chips and ingest them. If you have lead paint, then the baby is swallowing one of the most harmful chemicals out there.
- **Install fire alarms and fire extinguishers in your house**.
- **Take infant CPR**.
- **Always keep your eyes on the baby and never leave them unattended.**

Conclusion

The first few months of your baby's life are going to be stressful as well as joyous for you. You will be dealing with and encountering new issues like crying at night, breastfeeding, baby-proofing, feeding the baby, and learning about the chore it can be to leave the house. On top of that, you and your partner will feel stressed as you both deal with this new addition and the change it has brought into your lives. If you are lucky, you are one of the 80 percent of parents who do not have a colic baby. If you are not lucky, then you will suffer through many tired nights for the first three months.

The first three months of the baby's life are a time when their mind begins to take in everything that is around them. They begin to learn about the world, and you are there to help teach them about it. You will show them colors, shapes, textures, sounds, and sights that will leave them enthralled with everything you are doing. This is why it is important that you do everything that you can to nurture your baby's mind. By nurturing their mind, you help them later in life.

While you may feel stressed during this time, remember that you are on a journey with something amazing: a baby. The baby is new to the world, and they see the world in ways we do not. You can experience that with them; see the world through their eyes, and see it in a new light. You will see them smile, crawl, laugh, and cry. You will play with them, read to them, bathe them, feed them, and laugh with them. You will help them through these first three months by protecting them and showing that no matter what happens, you will always be there for them.

As a father, you are in a unique position to help make a big impression on a new life in this world. By working hard at it, showing love and attention, nurturing and encouraging them, you can create a productive member of our society.

These three months will not always be easy; you may not get much sleep, but when it is all said and done, you will look back on it as a happy time — one you may want to repeat again.

CASE STUDY: MAJOR RABI SINGH

Raised by his mother with his older brother, Major Rabi Singh enlisted in the Army straight out of high school. After several years with the Army, he met his wife, Carol, and now has four children.

What were your thoughts when you found out you were going to be a father?

I was the opposite of the unwed, unprepared pregnant teen. Carol and I deliberately delayed having children in order to strengthen our marriage first. After two years, we discussed when to begin and decided around fall 1994. However, we found out in May 1994 that she was already pregnant. Although the timing was a small surprise, we were fully prepared to have kids. I felt very happy and looked forward to our first child's birth. We found out about a month before I graduated college and received my officer commission. I also felt a burden of responsibility that would come my way eventually.

What was the most difficult transition during your partner's pregnancy?

For me, it was not really difficult since the baby changed her, not me. However, for what it's worth, our doctor told her that she did not weigh enough according to their charts and that she needed to gain weight. He gave her fattening tips, and she gained 10 extra pounds. We now realize that was a crock, and Carol noticed that after she lost her pregnancy weight, she never got rid of that extra 10 pounds.

Did you ever think you would be a father?

Yes. There was never a doubt, only a "When?"

What was the first thought to enter your head when the labor started?

Our oldest was overdue, so the doctor induced, which means that I was woken up in the middle of the night like on TV. That said, I do not have any clear memory of when her labor started, but I generally remember that it was exciting that day to know that "today is the day."

Did you find it difficult juggling the roles of father and soldier?

When my first child came, no, because the only overseas deployment was the Balkans. They never sent me because they only needed a few soldiers in my

CASE STUDY: MAJOR RABI SINGH

specialty, so I had essentially the same work schedule as the average civilian. I would not say that I struggled with being a father and soldier, but I did have to go through the same adjustment every father does. For example, trips took longer because you have to take care of the baby, put it down somewhere for a nap, etc. When I did end up deploying to the Middle East, the only downer I had was that my son was almost 2, and I would miss that entire year, which I could not gain back. My older kids would change, but the difference between 9 and 10 is not much, whereas I would miss a key part of my son's childhood.

When the baby was born, were you overwhelmed?

I was not, but my wife was. I would say I was irritated and got down at times because infants can be demanding. When a man is in a situation, it is easy to get blinders on and forget that the situation is temporary. When we had a 2-year-old and a newborn, an older friend reminded me that kids grow up and leave, and you can go out with your wife on a Friday night and have fun. I totally forgot that.

Describe the first few months of your baby's life and how it affected you.

It was cool just holding her. Once I had her, I had a love for her that sprouted within me. Girls tend to dream about having babies even as children, so for me as a man, it was an experience that I had not truly contemplated ahead of time. I enjoyed showing her off and was very proud of her. Like many dads, I made sure the car seat was in properly and drove her home from the hospital at 15 miles under the speed limit.

What were some of the games you would play with your children when they were babies?

I would help her do some Army physical-fitness type-training. I would move her arms and legs like she was running, doing jumping jacks, flutter kicks, etc.

What is your favorite part of being a father?

Tough question. I would say it is seeing them developing into independent, intelligent people who love others and serve Christ.

CASE STUDY: MAJOR RABI SINGH

How do you think your situation, being a soldier, differs from other fathers?

The obvious addition to deployments would be the fact that we are closer to death than the average civilian, so I believe I think more about spending time with them than the average civilian. For example, I am currently in a one-year military school here in Kansas and have already been told that when I leave, I am going to a deploying unit. So I live and schedule my life this year knowing that I will go to the Middle East for a year next year. For the average civilian, this year will not be much different than next year.

CHAPTER 7

From Three Months
to Two Years

"Children are born true scientists. They spontaneously
experiment, and experience, and re-experience again.
They select, combine, and test, seeking to find order in
their experiences — 'Which is the mostest? Which is
the leastest?' They smell, taste, bite, and touch-test for
hardness, softness, springiness, roughness, smoothness,
coldness, warmness: they heft, shake, punch, squeeze,
push, crush, rub, and try to pull things apart."

- Richard Buckminster Fuller,
American architect and author

Beyond the first few months of the baby's life — and up to
a year or two after the baby was born — you are going to
have several great experiences together. There are so many things
that you can do with your baby when they are under 2 years old.
You can help them walk, teach them to speak, take care of them
while they are teething, give them their first haircut, introduce
them to solid foods, and help them with potty training.

During the next 21 months of your baby's life, from the age of three months to two years, you are going to go through changes with your baby. There will be good times, and there will be bad times, but it will all be new to you and your baby. Your baby will experience new things, and you will experience those same things with them in a fresh way.

The next 21 months are a marvel in your baby's life and a point in your life that you will never forget for as long as you live.

Playing With the Baby

One of the most important things you can do with your baby, from when they are a newborn up to later in life, is to play with them. With your baby, playing is a great way to nurture their mind and create a strong bond that will help foster a strong relationship for years to come. There are many games that you can play with your baby that are meant to keep them interested and help them learn about the world around them, as well as about you, their father.

Four to Six Months

During this stage of the baby's life, there are several great games that you can play with them. Naturally, these will take a lot of involvement from you:

1. One great game is to take the baby's natural desire to pick up things and help them improve on that skill. Put several of the baby's toys on the floor, and then hold the baby face down so that the baby is resting on your forearm. Then, lower the baby while you make machine noises so that the baby

is directly over top of the pile. When they are low enough, let the baby pick up items and then, after about five to ten seconds, begin lifting the baby up. If the baby grabbed a toy, make a big fuss about it so that they get excited to pick up another toy when you lower them down over the toys again. This is a great activity that helps to build their depth perception, motor skills, and eye-hand coordination.

2. A great activity that requires your supervision, but which you can do while you are working or cleaning, involves a balloon. By tying a balloon to the baby's leg (loosely), you will be able to watch the baby get enthralled by the floating thing attached to their leg. The baby will laugh and get excited at this, and that will only increase when they move their leg and realize that moving their leg moves the balloon. The baby will begin to understand what is going on and have a lot of fun with it. This game builds their body awareness, reasoning skills, and eye-foot coordination. You should not use rubber or latex balloons if you do this.

3. You can put on a great animal shadow/puppet show for your baby with nothing but a flashlight and some cutouts of animals. Put the baby in the crook of your arm and turn off the lights. Then, with the flashlight, shine the light on the wall and move the cutouts of the animals in front of the flashlight to project the shadow on the wall. Name the animals as you do this and make animal noises. The baby will love this game, and it helps to foster a great bond with you because they are lying so close to you. This game will help their depth perception, language development, and visual discrimination.

4. One great game that we all know is the foot game of "This Little Piggy." This is a great game for your baby because it will help them learn about their body, as well as help their language development with your singing. All you have to do is gently grasp their big toe and say, "This little piggy went to market" and grab each successive toe one at a time and say, "This little piggy stayed home," "This little piggy had roast beef," "This little piggy had none," and, "This little piggy cried 'Wee, wee, wee' all the way home." On the last one, run your fingers up the body of your baby, tickling them gently. The baby will begin to anticipate the tickling at the last toe if you do this a few times, and they will start giggling before you have even started to tickle them.

5. A good way to help strengthen your baby's arms and body is with a baby hand game. Have your baby lie down on their back, or even in a sitting position. Then, let them grasp your fingers or hands. Once they have, say "One, two, three — up we go!" and pull the baby up to a sitting position if they are lying down, or a standing position if they are sitting. Soon enough, your baby will start to anticipate being pulled up, and you will not have to do much as they pull themselves up under their own power. This helps them learn about cause-and-effect.

6. A good way to help your baby learn about voices, tones, rhythms, and speech is with a voice game. You start by saying something easy like "Ah." When your baby says "Ah" after you, you congratulate them with a tickle. Do this a few times, and then say something easy like "ooooh." When your baby does the same, congratulate them again. Before you know it, the baby will begin to match you eas-

ily and even start to say entire words, even if they do not understand the context of the words yet.

7. Sound games are very important to help your baby learn about music and rhythm. This is an easy game to play. All you have to do is sing a song and bounce the baby on your lap to the beat of the song. For fast-paced songs, clap your hands and have them clap their own, and for slower songs, you can rock them back and forth.

8. To help develop your baby's problem-solving skills while playing a fun game at the same time, you can hide their toys. Just take some of their toys, put them on the floor and then put each toy under a towel one at a time. Ask your baby, "Where is the ball?" Then, you pull off the towel and say, "There is the ball!" After only a few times, you will notice your baby is grabbing at the towel before you even have a chance to say, "Where is the ball?"

Seven to Nine Months

During this stage, your baby will be able to take a more direct approach to the games, even playing by itself while you keep an eye on it. These games will naturally also help to fuel their development as a child and create a strong bond between the two of you.

1. Your baby may be a budding artist, and what better way to encourage that growth than with a unique kind of painting. Take some containers of baby food that are different colors and put them in front of your baby at the table. Then, show them what they need to do by taking some of the food in your hand and smearing it on the big cloth or paper in front of the baby. The baby will then begin to

create its own painting by using the food. The great thing about this is that the baby can also eat the food while they paint. Naturally, do this activity before you give them a bath because they are going to need it after they are done. This activity helps their creativity, while also building their motor skills and hand-eye coordination.

2. If you want to help build your baby's problem-solving skills, then you can teach them Three-Cup Monte. Put three large cups in front of the baby, and put a small ball under one of the cups. First, have the baby point to the cup with the ball under it even if you have not moved the cups. Once they do this a few times, start to slowly move the cups around and have the baby choose the cup that houses the ball under it. This is a great activity because not only does it build problem-solving skills, it also helps their visual memory and teaches them that even though an object cannot be seen, it can exist. This is the concept of object permanence.

3. A good activity for both you and your baby is to put your baby in a basket with their stuffed animals and toys and put a pillow behind them. Then, you can push or pull the basket with your baby and their stuffed animals in it around the house. Make sure you make train noises as you move the basket around. One neat idea is to put stuffed animals at various spots along the route so that you can stop and add some stuffed animals to the train and take some off. The baby will love this game, and it can help to build their sequential thinking and role-playing skills as well.

4. Your baby is going to be crawling a lot at this age and that presents several more game ideas for you and your baby. One involves putting down different items for your baby

to crawl over. You can put down a welcome mat, bath mat, a towel, blanket, clothes, and even a pillow. If you do this outside, you can even use a patch of grass. Then, you crawl with your baby across these items and describe the texture. When they crawl on the welcome mat, you say "rough," and when they crawl across the towel you say "soft." This will help your baby learn the differences among these items.

5. To develop your baby's verbal and social skills with a game at this age, you can use the telephone. Just pretend to talk into the phone, then hand the phone to the baby. The baby will begin to talk into the phone. Try talking to the baby through your cell phone into a landline.

6. Your baby is at the right age where you can carry them and fly them around the house pretending that they are an airplane. Flying around the house will be a delight for your baby, and they will likely squeal with happiness. Be careful, of course, and make sure you bring them in for a nice and easy landing.

7. Singing with your baby at this age is a great way to help them develop their listening and verbal skills. One song that is perfect for your baby is "Old MacDonald Had a Farm." When you sing this song, pick up a stuffed animal that matches the name of the animal in the song. Make sure you make the noise of the animal and then encourage your baby to do the same so they can learn by association about animals and their sounds.

Nine to 12 Months

Once your baby is reaching roughly the age of one year, the number of games you can play with them, and their involvement in it, can increase greatly. You will have a lot of fun with your baby during this age, and the games you play will further help their development that you began in the previous months.

1. One game that your baby will enjoy that stems from the plane game we described earlier is the hammock game. Take a blanket or towel and place your baby in the center of the towel. Grasp the two corners (head and feet) firmly so that the baby is secure, but so they can also see through the crack in the center. Then lift the bag gently, and slowly swing it back and forth in an area where there is no danger of the baby hitting anything. This game will develop your baby's trust in you and spatial awareness, while at the same time giving your arms a good workout.

2. Your baby will be starting to walk at this stage, even if it is with some assistance. A great way to help your baby with its walking skills is to give it a push cart walker and put the baby on one side of the room. Then, stand at the other side of the room with a sheet and begin making noises like "Toro, Toro!" so the baby begins to move toward you. Then, once the baby has made its way to the sheet, you can swoop the sheet over their head and go to the other side of the room to start the process over again. This is a great game for your baby because it builds their balance and coordination, while at the same time improving their walking skills.

3. A good bath time game is to give the baby a sponge to play with. This game helps build their body awareness. When they hold the sponge, say, "Do you want to wash your arm?" and help them sponge their arm. Do this a few times, and they will wash their arm on their own. Do this for their legs, belly, head, and other arm. It is also a great way to teach them to bathe themselves.

4. Your baby will begin to start speaking basic words and making signs around this age, and any games that nurture this are very important steps in that process. Play word games with your baby where you point to items and say their name, and then have the baby say the same name. The more you do this, the quicker your baby will get with making the associations between the object and the words.

5. The baby is going to be moving a lot by this stage, so one good game is to make yourself a jungle gym. Lie on the floor on your back, and let the baby move around on you, jumping on your chest and being lifted into the air by you. It is a great workout for you, and the baby will love the fun time playing with their father.

6. During this age, it can be time to start getting the baby interested in music. One way to do this is to make a homemade drum and show the baby how to hit it to make different sounds. The baby will have a lot of fun with this because babies love to make noise. Although you may find it a bit hard to take after an hour or so, it is a good game for your baby. Who knows: Letting your baby play the drum in the living room may help them become the next Keith Moon.

7. At this age, the baby will be old enough that they can move around on their own without you watching their

every move. This allows you to play a game of Peek-A-Boo where you lie on the floor with a blanket over you. Let your baby find you and when they find you, congratulate them and make a big fuss about them discovering you. Then you do the same with the baby. They will have a lot of fun with this basic form of hide and seek.

Preparing for Walking

During the first year of your baby's life, your baby is going to progress through several stages of locomotion. First, the baby will start to pull itself along the ground with its stomach touching the ground. Within a couple of months, the baby will begin to crawl along its hands and knees or its hands and feet. However, between the ages of nine to 12 months, the baby will begin taking its first steps on its own. By the time the baby is 14 to 15 months, it will be walking quite well on its own. Begin with certain exercises to help the baby develop the ability to walk in due time.

- In the first few weeks of the baby's life, you should hold the baby upright under their arms. The baby will let its feet dangle and push against the ground with their feet. While this may seem like it is walking, it is not. The baby does not have strong enough legs yet to support its upper body, and it will just fall over. You have to remember that the baby spent nine months in fluid, and like someone who has spent nine months in a wheelchair not using their legs, they will not be strong enough to use them when the time comes to stand up. Within two months of the baby's birth, they will stop pushing against surfaces when you hold them up.

- When the baby is roughly five months old, you can balance them on their feet on your lap. The baby will bounce up and down and actually have quite a bit of fun doing that. This also strengthens the baby's legs and begins them on the road to walking, as well as rolling over, sitting, and even crawling if it has not started yet.

- Once your baby has reached eight months, they will be trying to stand on their own by propping themselves up on something. When they first start doing this, they will be hanging onto the edge — usually something like the couch — and not moving. However, within a few weeks, they will be moving upright while holding onto the furniture. There will be times at this point when they let go and begin to move along the furniture without touching it.

- Between the age of ten months to 1 year, the baby will begin to bend its knees and therefore learn how to sit after standing. This is actually a difficult thing for the baby to learn. For the bulk of its life, it has just fallen onto its butt when it wanted to sit. Now, it will start bending down to sit without falling.

- Also during this period, the baby will be standing, bending over, and squatting. The baby should also be able to walk while holding your hand, but its real first steps across the room are still weeks away. One interesting point about this is that the baby will not walk normally, but rather on its tip-toes before it walks on the balls of its feet due to their evolving abilities. Once the baby has hit 13 months, it should be walking on its own. Roughly 75 percent of all toddlers are walking on their own at this point; however, do not worry if they are not. Some children take as long as 17 months to walk on their own. The important thing is that you help them with their development by aiding their walking and strengthening their body.

While you may think that this is the end of the road in walking development, it is far from the case. For the next few months, your baby will continue to develop its walking ability. Here is a quick rundown of the milestones that lay ahead after 13 months:

- At 14 months, your child should be able to stand on its own and will even start walking backward as well as forward.

- At 15 months, your child will be walking without any problems and will begin to push and pull their toys along with them. This is a favorite activity of children this age, so try to have those types of toys around.

- At 16 months, your child will begin looking at the stairs as a mountain to conquer. As humans, we have a desire to conquer everything around us, and for babies, one of the biggest challenges is stairs. While your baby will be looking up at the stairs, they will not be walking up them for a few more months.

- At 18 months, your baby will be walking up and down the stairs with your help. They will also discover the joy of climbing on everything in the house, including stairs. They will be kicking things and even dancing to music by this point.

- By their second birthday, they should have no problem walking, and they will be getting used to jumping up and down.

So, how do you get your baby walking and progressing in a manner that will get them on the fast track to walking and running? When your baby first starts to make their steps toward walking, they will most likely fall on their butt. Instead of going and picking up your baby, you should show them how to bend their knees so they can sit without falling over. Then, let them do it themselves. Show them how to stand up on their own from the sitting position. Doing this a few times will train your baby how to walk, sit, and stand on their own without your picking them up.

The best way to encourage your baby to walk is to stand or kneel in front of him or her. Hold out your hands and have them walk toward you. If you can buy a toy that allows the baby to use it as support as they walk, then all the better. This will teach them to walk on their own, albeit with some assistance. It will also strengthen their legs so that they will be able to walk on their own in no time at all.

Here are some tips to get your baby walking beyond what we have already mentioned:

- Walkers and jumpers at an early age may seem like the great solution to helping a baby walk, but they actually hinder it. When a baby is in a walker, it is sitting, not standing. This can delay the development of the muscles that are needed for a baby to start walking. When the baby decides to start walking, the feeling of standing will not feel natural as a result of the walker.

- You should provide daily encouragement to your child to get them walking. Shower them with praise to show them what a good job they have done.

- Do not hold your baby by the hands unless they are walking on their own. Instead, hold them by the torso; this will be more natural than walking with their hands in the air.

- Until the baby is walking outside, do not bother with shoes. Our feet are perfect for walking, and when you use shoes, you are not letting the feet develop the way they should for walking. If you worry about the baby walking on cold floors, you can put socks on them. Make sure these socks will not cause them to slip, though.

- Whenever you can, take your baby to different places to walk so they can feel the textures of what they walk on. Babies love to feel textures, especially on their feet. Take them to walk on grass, sand, carpet, wood, tiles, and linoleum. These new experiences will give your baby a drive to walk more and more.

Naturally, because your baby will be falling over a lot, you should go around the house and put padding on all sharp corners. This is especially true in the living room, where you will have to put padding on the tables, shelves, and even on the sides of the walls or in doorways. The last thing you want is for your baby to be excited that it is walking, then to fall and hit its head and decide that walking simply is not worth the pain.

Time to Speak

From seven months on, your baby is going to begin saying its first words. Usually the first words it will say will be very simple words that they have picked up listening to you and your partner speak. Often, the first word is something like "dada." While this will put a smile on your face, know that "dada" is one of the basic, babbling syllable combinations that a baby will speak. The baby will say it to everyone, even other men, which can be a bit disheartening. Babies learn in categories; therefore, dada is all men, rather than just you. If the baby says "dada" three times and points at you, or a picture of you, then that would qualify as their first true word.

Here is a rundown of what your baby will be doing at various stages of their language development:

Birth to Six Months

During this stage of language development, the baby will begin to cry when they hear loud or strange noises. They will also begin to make a variety of sounds beyond cries, including gurgles and coos. When you make noises, they will respond by smiling, making sounds, and staring at you as they listen in an effort to learn what you are talking about. Also at this stage, when they start crying, they may stop if you are talking to them in a soothing and pleasant voice. The baby will make sounds and noises back to you in response to your own talking to them.

Six Months to One Year

During this stage, the baby will begin to use simple words and understand their context. They will use words like "dada," "up," "bye," "hot," and "no." They will also begin to understand simple sentences like "Find mommy" and "Do not touch." Babies will make a great deal of sounds during this stage, imitating you and your actions and even singing along with you while you do something. They will imitate sounds you make, like coughs, kisses, and even tongue clicks. As they begin to understand more about speech, they will begin pointing and reaching to tell you what they want, which is a useful and simple form of sign language.

One Year to 18 Months

During this age, your child will be able to point to pictures of common objects, people, and animals and tell you what they are. They will also be able to learn to use items in a logical manner. You may find them driving the truck on the floor rather than just holding it and moving it through the air. The toddler will also use gestures and sounds to let you know what they want. You may find them pointing to the fridge and saying "appa duce" for "apple juice." During this age, your child will also be jabbering a lot as he or she discovers more and more about language. By this time, they will also have learned about their own body and will be able to identify their hair, mouth, eyes, and more with words. Typically, they will have a vocabulary of about 50 or more single words.

Normally, your child will not develop an adult form of communication (complex sentences, hundreds of words in vocabulary) until around age 6.

So, how can you help to encourage the development of your baby's speech? There are a variety of ways.

- When your baby begins making noises, even if it just seems like baby babbling, join in the talk and make it a conversation. You can really talk about anything, but over time you will begin to notice that your baby waits for your response to its babbling before it says anything themselves.
- Each day, walk around the house with your baby and point to various items and say their name. Point to the couch and

say "couch;" point to the fridge and say "fridge." Even talk about what those items are. Say, "The couch is where we sit" and "The fridge is where we put food." You do not have to be too specific yet, but doing this will help your baby learn by association.

- According to various studies, babies learn language easier when it comes in the form of rhyme or even a simple rhythm. When you are reciting simple rhymes, be sure to emphasize and elongate the words that rhyme.

- If your baby points to the fridge and says "dada," do not despair, just applaud them. The baby is now starting to put words to objects, and while it is wrong, you should applaud them and say, "Yes, that is a fridge. Fridge! Great job!"

- There are several books that can help your baby learn how to speak properly. These books come in the forms of lift-the-flap books, books with zippers, touch-and-feel books, and even button books. These will build your baby's vocabulary while improving their hand-eye coordination.

- Holding and cuddling your baby will help them bond with you, and when you talk with them while doing this, it will help them learn as well as feel safe.

- If your baby smiles to you or makes a sound, always acknowledge it.

- When you are talking to your baby, especially when they are younger, you should use short sentences. These will be easier for the baby to understand and learn.

- When your baby makes a sound or action, copy it after they do it. This will help the baby learn by seeing what you are doing and associating it with what they just did.

- If your baby says something like "couch," then you should say "couch sit" to help them learn more about what they are identifying.

- Look at and talk about pictures with your baby to help them learn about what each picture means.

It is very important, no different than helping them learn to walk, that you work to help your child learn more about speech so that they can develop a better ability to talk and recognize words in their proper context. This can be a lot of fun as you take the role of teacher to help your child learn about the world around them and how to express themselves using body language and verbal language.

Switching to Solid Foods

Within the first year, you are going to begin moving your baby away from breastfeeding or formula and toward more solid foods. This can be a difficult transition for everyone involved. For you, it means trying to get your baby to eat something it may not want to, and for the baby it can mean stomach discomfort due to a change in diet. On top of that, you may also find that the soiled diapers of your baby get bigger and more frequent as the change of diet takes effect.

There are several schools of thought as to when this change in diet from liquid to solid foods should be made. Some parents start their children quite early, while others wait until even the first year. It may be messy, it may be aggravating, but the switch must be done and the earlier you do it, the easier it will be to make the transition.

Generally, you can switch your baby to solid foods after six months, as long as your baby is ready for it. There are several ways to know when your baby is going to be ready for solid food. Look for these signs:

- The baby must be able to hold its head upright for an extended period of time.

- Babies have an extrusion reflex that causes them to push food out of their mouths with their tongues. Once your baby stops having this reflex, they will be better able to keep food in their mouths and swallow it.

- In order to swallow their food properly, babies need to sit upright properly.

- An interesting fact about babies is that their digestive systems develop in sync with the mouth and tongue. As a result, your baby needs to be able to move food to the back of their mouths with their tongue, and they also have to learn to chew food without drooling as much. The baby will start teething around this time, so it provides you with a good visual aid to know when this stage starts.

- When the baby has doubled its birth weight, or weighs at least 15 pounds, it may be ready for limited solid food.

- If your baby seems to be hungry a lot, even after as many as ten feedings in a day, then it may be time to switch them to solid food.

- If the baby seems very curious about what you are eating and keeps looking at what you are eating, then it may be time to start switching their diet.

Introducing Solid Food

When you decide to start the baby on solid food, it is a good idea not to start them on steaks or other hard food. You should gradually get the baby ready for solid food by introducing easy foods for them to eat and digest. A good start would be rice cereal, which is gluten-free and contains fewer allergenic items than other foods. Once the baby has begun to eat rice cereal, you can begin giving them dry cereal with breast milk mixed into it so that it is partly liquid. Try and use a rubber-tipped spoon so that the baby does not hurt themselves or their gums when they are first learning to eat with a spoon.

When you do start feeding the baby solid foods and making that transition from breast milk, make the solid food feeding a once a day on a schedule that is convenient for you and your baby. However, you should make sure you do not schedule the feeding when your baby is cranky. You will notice that the baby does not eat much at first, but eventually they will begin to like the food and the experience and eat more. The important thing is to remain patient with them as they learn about how to eat solid food.

One question many parents have at first is: How will you know that your baby is full? The baby cannot say "I'm full," but they can give you indications that they do not want to eat anymore. If your baby leans back in their chair and turns their head away from the food, it may be that they are full and do not want anymore.

The other most common question is: Should you do a cold turkey switch from breast milk to solid food? The answer to this is no, because your baby will still need the nutrients of breast milk until they are about one year old. Studies have found that solid food cannot replace the vitamins, iron, and protein that can be found in breast milk within that first year.

Types of Food to Introduce

After you have let the baby try rice cereal and dry cereal mixed with breast milk, it is the right time to begin introducing new foods. You should wait about three days between each type of food, and you should keep an eye out for the signs of allergic reactions to foods. These reactions include a bloated stomach, more gas, a rash, and even the runs.

Once you have moved beyond the cereals, you can begin giving your baby strained and mashed fruits and vegetables. After this, move on to finely chopped table foods — meat and other sources of proteins — that are important for the development of your baby.

Other good foods to start with include:

- Sweet potatoes
- Squash
- Applesauce
- Bananas
- Carrots
- Oatmeal
- Pears
- Peaches

Yellow fruits are easier for your baby to digest, according to some experts, but other experts feel you should start on green foods. In reality, it is up to you and the baby as to what kinds of foods you use. If your baby likes the food, they will eat it; if they do not like the food, they will not eat it. Just remember to mash and strain the food so that your baby will not choke on it.

It can be trying at times to get your baby to eat a particular food. However, rather than forcing them to eat the food, just let them make the choice. Try again in a week or two, and you may find that your baby actually wants that food now.

During the entire process, your baby's stool may change color and smell when you switch to solid foods. It is normal for this to happen, but if you find that the stool is very firm, the baby may become constipated, and you should switch to more oatmeal, fruits, and vegetables and less rice, bananas, and applesauce.

A good menu for your baby throughout the day, once they have reached about eight months, is the following:

- Breast milk
- Cereal
- Yellow vegetables
- Green vegetables
- Fruit
- Protein like fish, cheese, and meat

While the baby is just learning how to eat, this does not mean that their early solid food days are not perfect for developing healthy eating habits that will help them later in life. By implementing these healthy eating habits, you will help your baby later in life.

- Watch for the signs that your baby is full. You do not want to overfeed your baby.

- Do not feed your baby food that they do not like; you will only create a power struggle over the food.

- Balance the baby's meals so there are carbohydrates, protein, fruits, and vegetables in the food.

- Fast food should be avoided completely.

- If you want your baby to eat something, do not bribe them with sweets or something along those lines. After they have had something to eat, give them hugs and kisses.

- Use a highchair to feed your baby in the kitchen rather than in front of the television.

Teething

With the introduction of solid foods for your baby, you will begin to notice that they start teething as well. Teething can be a trying time to go through because it will be uncomfortable for your baby and that may lead to crying, which will lead to you not getting much rest or relaxation through the entire period of teething.

There are several signs that teething has begun for your baby. Generally, teething will begin around six to seven months in age, and the symptoms can actually appear months in advance of the teeth actually appearing. If you find your baby is drooling uncontrollably, it may be a result of teething and the swollen nature of their gums during that time. Also, if your baby is irritated for apparently no reason, waking up every hour crying or gumming whatever they can find, then teething may be the cause of it. In addition, your baby may have red cheeks, a rash on their chin, diarrhea, fever, bleeding gums, and a refusal to eat even when they are hungry.

As painful on your mind and hearing as this time can be for you, it is much more painful and irritating for your baby. They are literally having their teeth coming through their gums, which can be painful, and they do not realize what is happening or why. To help you and your baby through this ordeal of teething, here are some tips:

- You should try and numb the gum when you can. Putting a wet washcloth in the freezer so that it will freeze and then letting the baby chew on it is a great idea. The cold cloth on their gums will soothe your child. Another option is to put ice cubes into a blender and mix it with some mashed-up food. You do not want to give your baby a full ice cube as they may choke on it.

- You can put pressure on your baby's gums by gently pressing your clean finger on their gums and massaging the gum. If you do not have time to keep your finger in your baby's mouth for 10 hours, you can buy toys that do the same thing and will relieve the pain.

- You can also get medication for your baby to help with the teething. No, we are not talking about painkillers, but homeopathic teething tablets are a great choice for your baby when they are teething. These tablets are not drugs at all and are perfectly safe for your baby. You can also put teething gel on your baby's gums. These gels will numb the gums and provide some relief to your baby as a result. If you do numb the gums with a teething gel, do not do it

while they are breastfeeding, or else you could make suck-
ling difficult for your baby.

- Because drooling is common with babies who are teething, it is important that you protect the neck from it. Drool
can cause dryness and irritation on skin that is constantly
wet from it. This is often called drool rash, so make sure
you wipe away drool before it starts running down the
chin and cheeks and onto the neck.

- The stress of teething can actually make the entire process
worse than the pain. To remedy this, have soft music playing for your baby, talk to them, and massage them as well.
You can give your baby some very weak chamomile tea
as well to help them sleep while at the same time cooling
their mouth with the tea. Some parents even put a drop
of rum on the baby's gums to dull the pain. Some experts
frown on this, but you are only putting rum on the head
of a Q-tip®, so there is no danger to the baby, and it can
relieve the pain.

Caring for the Teeth

Once the teeth start coming in, you will need to begin helping
the baby care for them. When teething starts, you will be running
a clean and damp washcloth along your baby's gums every day
to help keep the gums clean and to prevent a buildup of bacteria
from occurring.

When your baby's teeth begin to appear, you can switch to a soft-
bristled toothbrush that fits on your fingertip. There are types
made especially for toddlers. It is important that you do not use
toothpaste. The reason is that toothpaste should not be swallowed,

and since babies do not learn to spit until the age 2 or 3, they will not be able to get rid of the toothpaste, so use water instead.

Around age 1, you should take your baby for their first dental appointment. By beginning a regular habit of childhood dental care, you can ensure that your child has a lifetime of healthy teeth and gums.

Teething is a trying time for both you and the baby. However, by implementing these tips and working to find ways to make it better, both you and your baby will get through it easier. The great thing about teething is that it will eventually pass, and your baby will find having teeth is well worth the pain of growing them.

The First Haircut

Eventually, the baby's hair in its first year will grow so long that you will need to cut it. You may not need to cut all of it, but the bangs will have to be cut if they are interfering with the baby's vision. This can be a nervous time for a parent because they may not like the idea of themselves, or anyone else, going to their baby with scissors near their face. Your baby may also find it to be a stressful event since they have never experienced it before.

There are salons that will cut baby hair, but many parents choose not to take their baby to a barber because of time, money, or the worry of a lot of crying in public.

When you are cutting the hair on the back of the head, you should put the baby in a high chair facing the television or in front of your partner as they do something to distract the baby. Stand behind the baby, and while using rounded scissors, cut from the center of the head, out to the right and left. Only do a small amount at a time because you want to be able to cover up errors if they happen. If you try and take it all off right away, you will only cause yourself problems.

When you are cutting the bangs, you need to be more careful. This is because babies will often move their heads and arms around when you are cutting their bangs. Therefore, you should cut your baby's bangs when they are asleep because they will not be moving around. If they are asleep in a stroller or car seat, all the better because they will then be at the right angle for you. Again, use scissors with rounded edges and ensure your hands and fingers are between the scissors and the baby's head. Have the hair come through the gaps between your fingers.

Potty Training

Many parents vary on when they are going to start potty training their children. Some begin working with them at 1 or 2 years old, while others wait as long as 3 before they start training their baby to use the toilet rather than diapers. It is unlikely you will toilet train before 1 year or even 18 months, but because this is an important step in your child's development, we will go over some of the steps that you will need to use when you do decide to toilet train.

There are several ways to get your child ready for the potty when the time comes.

1. You should try to make going to the potty fun for your child. One way this can be done is by making up a song

about going to the bathroom so that you and your child can sing it together when it comes time to go to the bathroom. The great thing about doing this is that before long they will be using the bathroom every time because they enjoy the experience and the song so much.

2. Reading to your child from the many different type of books that teach kids about using the toilet is a good idea. The most famous of these books is *Everyone Poops* by Taro Gomi, and it has helped generations of kids with the entire potty training process.

3. Using a timer is a good idea to help your child to remember to use the potty. By setting the time at one hour first, you will notice that your child will be using the bathroom with longer gaps of time in between. Once you notice that your child is not going to the bathroom every hour, you can begin increasing the time to two hours or so.

4. If you have a son, you can make going to the bathroom fun by putting colored ice cubes in the toilet, or even confetti. That way, they can aim and shoot for the targets and get rewards depending on how accurate they were. For boys this can help train them to use the toilet within a couple of weeks. For girls, you can get special water for the training toilet so that urine turns the water blue or another color. This makes the process more fun, and therefore, something they want to do.

5. Making your child feel proud after going to the bathroom is very important. After they use the bathroom, make sure you say what a great job they did or what a big boy or big girl they are for doing that. This praise can go a long way in helping your children get more at ease with potty training.

6. Let them put their hands into a surprise bag where you have a variety of inexpensive toys and stickers. They can grab something out of the bag as a reward for the great job they did in the bathroom.

7. Charting their progress can also be an effective way to get them ready for the potty. Put up a racetrack, a park path, or anything on the wall, and then each time your child uses the potty properly, you put up a sticker on the path in front of the last sticker. When the track is full of stickers, you can give your child a reward. That way, you give them a more meaningful reward, while at the same time giving them small rewards of the sticker on the track each time they use the potty so they can chart their own progress.

8. Kids are always interested in the flushing of the toilet. Make this a part of the process for learning how to use the potty. Each time they use the potty, let them flush the toilet to make everything disappear.

9. One thing many parents do is buy disposable training pants. The problem with these pants is that the child does not get uncomfortable if they go potty in them since they do not get wet. This can actually make potty training go on longer than it needs to. Resist the urge to buy these pants because if your child finds going in their regular pants uncomfortable, they will be more receptive to potty training.

There are several reasons why your child may not want to use the potty and may actually resist using it with all their power.

- They may be scared to sit on the potty chair because it is new, high up, and a change they may not be ready for.

Even the flushing of the toilet may scare them enough that they do not want to sit on the toilet.

- They are being pushed too fast to use the potty before they are ready to.

- There is inconsistent training, especially between Mom and Dad and their own different methods.

- If your child has been constipated, they may have had a painful bowel movement and that may make them not want to use the potty as a result.

- They could just be stubborn and not want to use the toilet and are in a power struggle with you for control over when they make a bowel movement.

- Children like attention, even negative attention, and they may even like the negative attention that they get from making accidents in their pants rather than using the toilet.

When you buy the potty for your child, let them decorate it with stickers and other items so that they can make it something they like, rather than fear. Even have your child sit on it while watching television with their clothes on so they get used to it, and the entire potty will not be such a strange mystery to them. Typically, only keep your child seated on the potty for a few minutes at a time, and you can even empty his dirty diapers into a potty chair so that they begin to understand what the potty is for. Eventually they will eliminate the middle man of the diaper and just use the potty themselves.

For your toddler to be toilet-trained, it needs to have bladder readiness. When babies are infants, they are not able to hold large amounts of urine within their bladder. As they grow older, their bladder begins to mature more so that they can hold larger amounts of urine between having to relieve their bladder.

Your child also needs to recognize that they need to empty their bladder or bowel. Under the age of a year, your child may not understand that they need to empty their bowels, and they just do it. The correlation between having to go and going in a certain place is not quite there yet and does not start appearing until about 18 months.

Your child also needs to be physically ready to use the toilet. They need to be able to walk well so they can get to and from the bathroom; they need to be able to pull up their own pants; and they need to be able to climb onto the toilet and off the toilet by themselves. One simple rule says that if your baby cannot walk yet, then it cannot be toilet-trained as a result.

Lastly, your child needs to be psychologically ready for the toilet. They need to be willing to go to the toilet and be bothered by having a dirty diaper. If they are not bothered by a dirty diaper, then they will not be willing to go on a toilet when they feel you can just change them instead.

The First Birthday Party

The first birthday for your baby is an interesting affair. Your baby will not remember the first birthday; they will not remember their first two or three, actually. They may cry at their first birthday, and they may hate it completely, so you may ask yourself: Why even bother?

Well, the first birthday is not so much for your baby as it is for you. It is the first big milestone for your baby (in terms of time, not events). Of course, you could choose not to celebrate the birthday, and your baby probably would not even notice or care that this milestone has passed. However, if you are like most parents, you will have a first birthday party, and if you do, there are some tips to follow to make sure both you and your baby enjoy it.

1. Try and ensure that the party is small. The more people there are, the more stressed your baby will be. Limit the party to you, your partner, your parents and her parents, and maybe a couple of aunts and uncles, but that is it. Any more than that and your baby may start to cry when everyone begins crowding around him or her.

2. If your baby naps at a certain hour, then you should not schedule their party during that time. Either there will be a meltdown, or the baby will just sleep through the party and you will not get that joy you were hoping for out of your baby's first party.

3. It may seem like a good idea to bring something you think your child may like to the birthday party, like a clown or a large mascot from a show they like, but this is a bad idea. When your child sees these people and creatures on the television, they are much smaller than the baby. When they see them in person, they are very large and can be quite frightening.

4. Even though the birthday is for your baby, the adult guests need to be taken care of. Most do not want to be at a first birthday party, so make sure you have things there to help

them enjoy the entire event and ensure they are coming back for birthday No. 2.

The gifts at the first birthday party are not essential. The baby will most likely enjoy playing with the wrapping and the box more than the actual toy. Let your guests know they do not have to bring a gift for the baby if they do not want to, but if they do, they are more than welcome to. This takes any obligation away from your friends and family for gifts, which can make the party much more enjoyable.

You should schedule the birthday party so it does not conflict with anything that your friends and family have planned. The baby does not care when the party is, so to keep your friends and family happy, and at the party, try not to schedule the birthday party during the Super Bowl or any other large event.

As for party games, anything that takes longer than a minute or two is out of the question due to the poor attention span of a 1-year-old. Therefore, party games should be something the adults can enjoy, too. Examples of these would include:

- How much frosting can the baby put on their face within two minutes?
- How long before the baby takes off their party hat?
- Which baby can crawl to a finish line in the living room the fastest?
- Which baby laughs first from having their feet tickled?

These games are simple, fun for the baby, and even fun for the adults at the birthday party.

For food, have a cake for everyone, appetizers, and maybe even some wine for the adults. You can even have a potluck, where everyone brings their own food to the party. That way you can turn the first birthday party into something that is also a party among your friends; it is win-win for everyone involved.

Restaurants

Despite your better judgment, you may want to go out for supper as a family with your baby. While this can often be a great experience, there is also the chance that your dinner, and that of everyone's around you, will be interrupted by crying and angry fits. Even if your baby is very well-behaved, you may still get dirty looks from your other restaurant-goers simply because you have a baby who may cry and ruin their dining experience. If anything, it can give you a nice secluded corner where no one else will want to sit around, which can work out for you.

If you do choose to go to a restaurant, look for one that has these items in it, which can be termed as baby-friendly items.

- Televisions to distract babies and even drown out their crying if they do.
- High chairs so your baby can actually sit comfortably and safely at the table.
- Any place that caters to kids, like Chuck E. Cheese®.
- Crayons so that your baby can at least draw and distract itself while you are eating, but make sure they do not eat the crayons.

As for the types of restaurant you should go to, try out these restaurants as a good bet:

- Mexican restaurants have an atmosphere that can be described as loud and casual, and some even have mariachi bands that can help to entertain your baby.

- Seafood restaurants are good as well, especially if you are sitting near the fish and lobster tanks so they can distract your baby.

- Sports bars are great because they have a high noise level that will mask any cry from your baby, and the televisions can keep them occupied. That all being said, it is best not to go on game night, but on a night where it will not be as busy.

- Chinese restaurants are good for taking the baby to because they have nice appetizers of crunch noodles for the baby to play with. Their rice dishes are also good for the baby to eat.

- Salad bars or buffets are good because there is no waiting for food, so you can shorten the entire restaurant experience to as little time as possible.

While these restaurants can be a great fit, you may still need to practice some tactful strategy to make the entire experience easier on yourself and others. Follow these tips to make it happen:

- Make sure you go early so that there are very few people in the restaurants. Going at 5 p.m. is a good idea. Those that are there probably will not care that much about the baby and will most likely be seated far away from you.

- Before you go to the restaurant, feed your baby. Yes, this seems odd, but a hungry baby at the restaurant means a stressful time for you until the food comes out. Moreover, the child probably will not eat anything from the kid's menu before the age of 1 as it will still be on baby food. Give your baby a bit of food before you go out and ask if you can have bread or crackers when you sit down, just in case the baby wants some.

- Where you sit makes a big difference. Near the kitchen not only can cause your baby to be stressed with all the traffic, but there is the danger that something may fall off a tray and onto your baby. Booths are not a good idea because the high chair will have to stick out into the aisle, which can cause bottlenecking if a lot of people go by. Have the baby sit by the window so they can be distracted, or have a place near the exit so that you can take the baby out if they begin to cry.

- Keeping your baby occupied is very important. Toys and books are a good idea because they will keep the baby's mind on the items in front of them, and not on the commotion around then.

- Babies like to pick up things up. What they pick up, they also like to throw. Unless you want to deal with an angry diner who just took a salt shaker to the head, you should set up a zone where there is nothing for the baby but what you want them to play with. This is your no-fly zone where there is no food or drinks. You would be surprised by how far a baby can stretch, so do not just rely on how long their arms are to create your radius.

- If you plan on going back to this restaurant again, make sure you tip well. For servers, it can be stressful to have a baby at a table, especially if that baby likes to make a big mess. Show you appreciate the server by giving them a tip that ensures they will want you seated in their section next time.

Going to Hotels

If you decide to travel, you may need to stay in a hotel. In this section, we need to address what to do when you stay in the hotel with a baby.

Hotels can be great places, especially if your baby is learning to walk. Long hallways have no clutter and plenty of room to move around, so by going for a walk with your baby through the hallways, you can give them much-needed training in walking without the worry that they are going to fall and hurt themselves on an object. Another great thing about this is that the more they walk with you in the hallway, the more tired they will be in the hotel room, and the quieter it will be for you and your partner.

The first thing you need to do is figure out where your baby will be sleeping. You probably do not want to lug their crib in the car and through the hotel, so you may need to think of some other options.

One option that many hotels provide for you is a portable crib. The only problem is that these cribs are usually poorly maintained and the mattresses have a lot of accidents left by other babies that have not been cleaned properly. The only other option beyond this is to have the baby sleep in the bed with you and your partner.

If the baby is sleeping in a portable crib, then it is important that you block the view of the bed from the baby. The reason is that if the baby wakes up in the middle of the night and sees you there, it may not want to go back to bed and will keep you up for the rest of the night. Just put some chairs between the crib and your bed with some towels over them and you should not have a problem.

If you want your baby to sleep properly, you need to make sure the room is conducive to sleep. You will want to keep the room dark, and sometimes lights outside of the hotel do not allow for this. Put up some hangers on the curtains to clamp them together and keep the lights from filtering into the room. Babies also like white noise, so you could create some by disconnecting the cable from the back of the TV set. Put a towel over the screen so that it is not too bright, and then turn on the television on a low volume. This will give the room a nice nightlight effect, and help your baby sleep with the white noise.

You are also going to need to baby-proof the room as well, no different than you did in the home. How can you do this so that you do not have to completely alter the entire room? It is quite easy.

- Let your baby crawl around the room, while you walk behind them. Grab anything near the baby and anything that may pose a threat to their safety. Put away the coffeemaker, iron, and hair dryer until you need those items.
- Cover up all the outlets in the hotel room with electrical tape, and use that same tape to keep all the drawers closed.

Use the baby's socks and tape to protect your baby from sharp corners on dressers and tables. Just fold the sock in half and tape it to the corner to provide some protection.

- To make sure the baby does not walk or crawl into the glass window or doors going out to the balcony, use the tape to put an 'x' on it so they can see there is something there.

- Make sure all the drape and blind cords are completely out of their reach of the baby. Bind them together so that only you and your partner can reach them.

- Secure all closet doors shut with pipe cleaner around the knobs to keep the baby from opening them.

- To also keep the baby safe, close the bathroom door and make it completely off-limits to the baby. If you find your baby can open doors, then you are going to need to keep them from opening the door. Putting a sock over the doorknob can keep this from happening, as they will not be able to get a grip on the doorknob.

Hotels can be a great new experience for you and your baby, but there are some things that you need to do to make everything safe for them. By baby-proofing the entire hotel room and helping the baby find the hotel room to be a relaxing environment, then you will not have any problems. It may go so well that the baby actually begins to enjoy staying in hotel rooms. Just remember to keep things safe and to keep an eye on your baby so that nothing happens that could hurt your baby, which would put a damper on any vacation.

The Airplane

There is the chance that you will have to travel by plane with your baby at some point. This is especially true if you and your partner are visiting family. With a baby, a two-hour plane ride can seem like eight hours sometimes, but there are ways to make the entire trip a lot easier on yourself and everyone else on the plane with you.

First, you will want to find a seat that is going to work best for you and the baby. When you book your flight, you can either book a seat for the baby or hope that there will be a free seat for you to put the baby in. If you book a seat for the baby, then book the middle seat so that it is between you and your partner. If you do not book a seat for your baby, then you should book the aisle and window seat for you and your partner, and then hope that the middle seat will be free. Generally, middle seats fill up last and most people will not want to sit between you and your partner if you have a baby, so they may seat themselves somewhere else if the plane is not full, giving you a free seat.

Bulkhead seats give the most legroom because you have a wall in front of you. Generally, that wall separates coach from first class and it provides you a lot of room for your legs and for your baby. Some airlines actually provide bassinets that attach to the bulkhead if you request it, so this is probably the best option for you.

You will not be able to sit in the emergency exit row because it is not allowed for parents with babies, but you can be seated near the bathroom. You will get some extra legroom for you and the baby, and your baby may be distracted by the constant flow of people in and out of the bathroom. If the baby starts crying, you can take them into the bathroom and play with them in front of the mirror as well.

Second, you are going to want your baby to sleep on the plane, and there are ways to make this happen. Follow these tips to get your baby sleeping during the flight:

- Take the red-eye flight so there is a better chance of your baby sleeping.

- Schedule the flight during your baby's naptime so there is a better chance they will sleep since they have been conditioned to sleep at that time.

- If you get to the airport early, you will be able to get the baby tired by walking them around the wide open areas and through the hallways of the airport. By the time you get to the plane, they will barely be able to keep their eyes open.

- If you really want to, you can give your baby some baby Benadryl® or Tylenol®. Before you do this, talk to your doctor first since you should not give medication to your baby without consultation.

Third, one of the toughest things for your baby to handle is the change in pressure in its ears. This can be painful for them, and that pain is translated into a lot of crying as the plane takes off and lands. Thankfully, there are ways to make this pressure change easier on your baby and yourself as well. When you are taking off or landing, have your baby on the bottle or breastfeeding. The reason is that they will be sucking and therefore adjusting the pressure in their ears as the plane rises or falls. It is just like when you chew gum during a flight to pop your own ears. If your baby is not in the mood for breast milk, then you can give them a pacifier to suck on.

Fourth, babies do not always do well with flying, just like people, and air sickness can come up in more ways than one. Babies do not know to use barf bags, and your fellow passengers in front of you may not appreciate the vomit hitting them in the back of the head. You may not be able to prevent the vomiting, but you can make it easier for yourself to clean up when it happens. Follow these tips:

- Bring four extra outfits for your baby in case they throw up a few times throughout the flight.

- Wear a windbreaker over your own clothes so that you can wipe away the vomit easily in the bathroom.

- Bring paper towels, wipes, and plastic bags to contain any vomit that may come out of your baby.

Fifth, your baby is going to need to go to the bathroom, and airplane bathrooms are not always the easiest place to change a baby's diaper in. The best way to change a diaper on a plane is with a towel over your lap or your partner's lap. Change the diaper and put the diaper in an air sickness bag. Be sure to apologize to those around you and hope that you do not have to change a diaper when the food is coming out, depending on if there is any on your flight.

Sixth, keeping your baby entertained is very important. For that reason, make sure you bring plenty of toys for your baby to play with and unwrap if they are new. A good rule of thumb is to use one toy for every half-hour of flight time. You can even make a puppet out of an air sick bag, or just let your baby play with your used boarding pass. If you have some nice and understanding people around you, they may want to entertain the baby as well with faces and funny voices. Generally, most people will be more than happy to make your baby smile.

Lastly, you will need to have something to hold your baby on the plane since you cannot hold them for the entire flight, especially if it is four hours or more. Many airlines allow you to bring a small stroller onto the plane, and you can use a car seat on the plane.

Conclusion

The first couple of years of your baby's life are incredibly important. During these years they learn some extremely important skills that will aid them throughout life. They learn to walk, run, speak, and understand the world around them. They learn to use the toilet, to listen to you and your partner, and they learn about playing, laughing, and enjoying life.

The first two years of a child's life are when many of the personality traits and mannerisms will begin to be developed, and that is why it is essential you provide your child with a loving and caring environment where their minds are free to soar around them.

As a father, playing with your baby is very important because it helps create a strong bond with your child that will continue for decades to come. In the next section, we will provide you with a reference guide to all the games that you can play with your baby. In addition to playing with them, you need to deal with some other important factors in your baby's early development.

You need to help them walk by being the person they can lean on when they have trouble standing. When they are learning to speak, you will be there providing them with a voice to learn from. You will show them the world of food that goes far beyond breast milk and formula, and you will help them through the troublesome times of teething and their first haircuts.

You will hold their hand as they go to the potty for the first time and shed the diaper forever, and you will throw a birthday party for them that celebrates the first year of their life, while you prepare for the coming years of joy and happiness with your baby.

These are important years for your child and for you, so cherish them as much as you can because when they are older and living outside your home, you will still remember them fondly.

CASE STUDY: MARC BLANCHETTE

Living in High River, Alberta, Marc and his wife, Victoria, have two children together.

Describe the feelings you had when you first found out that you were going to be a father.

At first I was scared, but happy in a way. I was 31 at the time and never thought I would have children.

When did the realization that you would be a father first come about?

I think once we had the final test done at the doctor's office. When he confirmed that there was a baby there, then I knew for sure that the baby was coming.

How much did you help your wife/partner during the pregnancy?

Between my full-time job and my Lions Club meetings, I think I was pretty supportive. I rubbed her back and filled her water jug during the night.

What were some of the changes in your life during the pregnancy?

She did not really feel pregnant until the last month, but there were a lot of late night runs for her craving: poutine (a Canadian dish of french fries covered with gravy and cheese).

Were you nervous about being a father?

Who would not be? You are about to bring a child into this world. It is a huge responsibility. But once I held my son for the first time, I fell in love with him instantly.

Describe your feelings when the labor first started and you had to get to the hospital.

I was scared as hell. It was too soon. She was only 27 weeks into the pregnancy. She was at her mom's 30 minutes away from our house, and I was at a Lions Club meeting another 30 minutes away from our house but in the other direction. We did not have a car, so I called my best friend when I got home, and he picked me up so we could go get my wife and bring her to the hospital. Because she was so early, they airlifted her by helicopter to a city seven or eight hours away.

CASE STUDY: MARC BLANCHETTE

What was the first thing you thought of when you held your newborn baby for the first time?

"Thank God he's all right," I said to myself. He was born 3 pounds, 4.5 ounces, at 27 weeks into the pregnancy, and in a town far away. I did not get to see him until they were flown back to our city. I almost cried the first time I held him. He was so tiny, and I loved him so much.

Did you ever worry about not being a good father?

I think everyone goes through that emotion. We have to live and learn and love our children no matter what. They are a part of us. And to watch them grow is the greatest thing on earth.

How many children do you want to have?

I wanted two and have been blessed with a son and a daughter.

SECTION 3

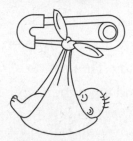

The Reference Guide

We have gone from the point of conception, through the three trimesters, and all the way to the first two years of your baby's life. This is a lot of information to take in, and not all can fit in those two sections. As a result, we have added this reference guide that will serve you for quick-lookups to help you learn about a variety of other things with your baby. You will learn about what you should do in case of illness with your baby, what games you can play with the baby, identifying dangers in the home, and understanding the relationship between you and your baby.

It is impossible to tell you absolutely everything that you will need to know about your baby. Thousands of books have been written about raising babies, and all of them cover different aspects, focus on different areas, and deal with babies in a different way.

We want to provide you with as complete a learning experience with your baby as possible. We want to help you learn about your baby, about what you can do to protect them, and how you can have a wonderful relationship that goes on for forever.

This reference guide may not cover everything you need to know, but it will cover the essentials that will give you a clear under-standing about other topics relating to your baby. Want to know what illnesses strike babies, what games you should play, and how you can protect them? This is the place to look.

So, let us begin filling in the gaps between the birth and those first two years with this reference guide.

CHAPTER 8

Illnesses
and Your Baby

To see helpless infancy stretching out her hands,
and pouring out her cries in testimony of dependence,
without any powers to alarm jealousy, or any guilt to alienate
affection, must surely awaken tenderness in every human
mind; and tenderness once excited will be hourly increased
by the natural contagion of felicity, by the repercussion
of communicated pleasure, by the consciousness of
dignity of benefaction.

- Samuel Johnson, English author

As much as we do not want it to happen, there is the chance
that your baby will get sick. While many parents will begin
to worry the minute they hear the cough, most illnesses are completely and easily treatable. The important thing is catching the
symptoms early and taking your baby to the pediatrician. With all
of these illnesses and conditions, if you feel you need to take your

baby to the doctor, do so immediately. And never give your baby medication without first consulting the doctor about it.

Chickenpox

A troublesome virus of children everywhere is chickenpox. This airborne disease is highly contagious. It is no surprise that in schools, the minute one child gets chickenpox, the entire classroom has chickenpox. Thankfully, once you have it, you will never have it again. The virus stays with you your entire life, and your immune system is what keeps a handle on it for you.

Symptoms

- Headache
- Fever
- Loss of appetite
- After two days, itchy, fluid-filled blisters will begin to appear on the baby's body

For children under the age of 10, having chickenpox is actually quite mild, versus if you have it as an adult. However, chickenpox can cause other more dangerous symptoms, depending on the baby's resistance to the virus.

- A secondary infection of the blister may occur if the blister is scratched. And the scratching of the chickenpox can actually lead to scarring.
- Newborns are at risk of having a serious and dangerous infection of chickenpox if the mother has never had the disease and therefore has no immunity.

Treatment

Chickenpox is a virus and therefore cannot be treated with simple antibiotics. Usually, all you can do is let a chickenpox infection go through its paces while you treat the blisters so that the baby has less of a chance of scratching the blisters and leaving scarring. To keep this from happening, be sure to trim the nails of your baby, or place scratch-mitts on babies to minimize the scratching.

Putting calamine lotion on the blisters will help to alleviate the itching. If you do not have calamine lotion, you can use baking soda mixed with a little bit of water to create a paste.

Fever

Sometimes your baby may develop a fever, and this can be extremely worrisome to a parent. In the past, fevers used to be the sign of a more dangerous disease coming into play, and it struck fear into the hearts of people before the use of antibiotics and modern medicine. These days, a fever is usually a symptom of something else, but a doctor can treat most fevers without much difficulty, and within a few days, it should pass. It is important to remember that a fever is not the enemy of your body or your baby's body, but simply the body fighting something. The reason for this is that most viruses and bacteria do well at normal body temperature and thrive even, so the body raises its temperature to fight the infection to limit the reproduction of the virus or bacteria.

That all being said, you should keep an eye on the fever and contact the baby's doctor if any of the following happen:

- If the temperature of your baby rises to 105°F

- If your child is under the age of six months
- If the baby has a stiff neck, cannot move an arm or leg, has a seizure, or is having labored breathing
- If the baby has an aversion to bright lights

When you are taking the temperature of the baby, use a rectal thermometer, as this will give you the most accurate reading by far.

Treatment

To treat a fever and reduce the fever to at least 101°F, you should contact your doctor. Remember, it is important to leave the fever to do its thing to help the body, but make sure that the fever is not too high; otherwise it can overcook the brain and cause brain damage.

Baby Allergies

When your baby develops an allergy, it is doing so because the immune system is overreacting. Essentially, it is overreacting to something that is completely harmless, and due to this overreaction, it causes an allergic reaction that is characterized by swelling, itching, and a rash.

Types of Allergies

For babies, these are the most common types of allergies that you will see develop, if any do.

- **Household chemical allergy:** Our lives seem to be full of chemicals, and our homes can have more chemicals in them than nearly anywhere else. Things like air fresheners carry particles so the scent can move throughout the room, which are full of chemicals as well. As a result, your baby can develop an allergy to household chemicals.

- **House dust mites:** Your home most likely has a lot of dust mites in it, even if you keep it clean on a daily basis. The dirtier your home is, the more likely your baby will develop this allergy.

- **Pollen:** If you go outside a lot in the spring, where there is a lot of pollen in the air, your baby may develop an allergy to weeds and even tree pollen. This is one of the most common forms of allergies.

- **Molds:** Many homes have mold to a varying degree, and mold can actually lead to mold allergies in babies. As with dust mites, the more mold you may have, the more likelihood there is that your baby will develop a mold allergy.

- **Pet hair:** Your baby getting a pet hair allergy can either come about because you do not have pets and they are not exposed to them, or because you do have pets with a lot of pet hair. Sometimes, early exposure to pet hair can actually keep your baby from developing pet hair allergies.

There are two very common allergies that babies can get. About one in every five children develops asthma or eczema, the same average for jaundice, all explained in following sections. If either you or your partner have had one of these, there is a good chance that your baby will also develop it.

Eczema

There are two different types of eczema. The first is infantile seborrhoeic eczema, which produces a greasy rash that will also look scaly. Roughly 50 percent of all babies will develop this before their first birthday. It will eventually go away with time and does not require any treatment.

The other type is atopic eczema, which causes dry and inflamed skin that is quite flaky. You can treat this with anti-histamines to sooth the skin. If you want to limit the chance of your baby developing atopic eczema, you can follow these tips:

- Vacuum your house on a daily basis. This will limit the number of dust mites that may be in the house.
- Have your baby wear cotton clothing and have cotton bedding to sleep on.
- Use non-bio washing powder on your baby.
- Keep your baby's nails short.

Atopic eczema will eventually clear up on your baby but not for about 12 to 13 years.

Asthma

When your baby develops asthma, they are developing an allergic reaction that causes their airway to swell shut, making it difficult for your baby to breathe. There is no way to cure asthma, but you can reduce the severity of the attacks by following these tips:

- Do not allow air fresheners or household chemicals in your home.
- Do not smoke.
- Vacuum on a daily basis. Be sure to vacuum their stuffed toys, curtains, and bedding.
- If you have a history of animal allergies, keep pets away from the baby.

- Have your partner breastfeed the baby for the first six months because this will provide the baby with antibodies they would not get if they only consumed formula.

Treatment

Treating asthma involves a puffer, which is a steroid inhaler. These are only used for older children and young adults. For a baby, there will be a small spacer that works like the inhaler.

Thankfully, there is a good chance that the asthma in your baby will disappear as they begin to grow older.

Baby Jaundice

One-fifth of all babies will experience baby jaundice, and thankfully it is not a serious condition and will usually pass within a week of its first symptom appearing. While many parents may begin to worry when they see the skin of their baby turning yellow, there is not too much reason to worry.

Symptoms

The skin of your baby will begin to get a yellow tinge to it, making your baby look as though it has a light suntan. If you have an African-American baby, then the yellow tinge will appear in the whites of the eyes.

The reason that jaundice can develop is because babies are born with high levels of bilirubin in their body. Bilirubin is the breakdown property of normal heme catabolism, which affects red blood cells. The yellowing of bruises is caused by bilirubin. The liver has to break this down for the body, but it can take about a week or more for the breakdown to occur. Thankfully, your baby will experience no pain or discomfort when they have this condition.

Treatment

If you want to break down the chemical sooner rather than later, you can expose your baby to more sunlight. Sunlight will help to break down the chemical along with the liver. If you are not able to get out into the sunlight (perhaps it is winter), then you can have your baby under bright fluorescent lights for a set period during the day. Do not allow your baby to get sunburned though! As with other diseases, breastfeeding can help to treat the jaundice and get the baby through that week of yellow eyes and skin quickly.

There is the chance that the symptoms may persist longer than two weeks. This is rare, and if it does happen, you should consult your doctor to find out what can be done to alleviate the jaundice.

Group B Streptococcus

Roughly 700 babies a year develop Group B Streptococcus (strep), or GBS, and roughly 100 of those babies will die from it in the United States. Of the 600 that survive, many will suffer problems that will exist for many years.

The reason babies will get this disease is because their immune systems are still quite weak, and roughly 30 percent of people carry the GBS virus without it causing any problems. Even if the mother has the GBS virus, though, there is only a 50 percent chance she will pass it on to the baby, and only 1 percent of the babies that get the virus will actually develop the disease.

Therefore, it is very hard to diagnose and treat because you do not know really if your baby is going to have it or not. However, if you meet any of the following criteria, there is a chance that your baby may develop GBS:

- If the birth is premature at about 37 weeks or sooner
- If the mother has a high fever during labor
- If membranes are ruptured 18 hours or more before delivery begins
- If there is a positive result on any test for GBS during the pregnancy

Meningitis

When there is an inflammation of the membranes around your baby's brain and spiral cord, it is usually meningitis. Now, this usually sounds much worse than it actually is. If it is viral meningitis, then it is actually very mild and usually does not require you to get any medical treatment for your baby. However, if your baby develops bacterial meningitis, it is a completely different story. This is life-threatening to your baby — and adults — and you should take them to a hospital almost immediately. With bacterial meningitis, children under the age of 5 are most commonly affected, and some of those children will die as a result of bacterial meningitis.

Meningococcal bacteria are the most common causes of bacterial meningitis. The amazing thing is that most of us carry these bacteria in our bodies without a problem. It is found in our noses and throats and is passed by kissing, sneezing, and coughing. It is when the bacteria make its way into the bloodstream, which is rare, that your baby will get meningitis. While it is rare to get this, it is important to know the symptoms so that you can take your baby to the doctor if you begin to notice any of them.

Symptoms

Look for these symptoms:

- Temperature above 99.5°F
- There is a difficulty waking the baby
- The baby stares for long periods of time at nothing
- The baby has an aversion to bright lights
- The baby develops a stiff neck
- Difficulty breathing
- Breathing is fast
- Shivering
- Vomiting
- Cold hands and feet
- There is a purple-red or brown rash on the baby
- The soft spot of the baby located on the head is bulging up
- The skin of the baby is pale or blue
- There is a lot of crying and wailing from the baby for no reason
- The baby has jerky movements of its limbs and a stiff body

If you begin to see any of these, take your baby to the doctor so that you can get a proper diagnosis, and treat the bacterial meningitis to keep your baby from suffering.

Measles

Usually arising in late winter and early spring, measles is an infectious viral disease that can cause a large multitude of symptoms. Typically, the measles will last about ten to 14 days on average. Like chickenpox, once your child has the measles, they are immune to it for the rest of their life.

Symptoms

The symptoms of measles are usually the following:

- Fever of 105°F
- Conjunctivitis
- Rash
- Runny nose
- Coughing
- Sensitivity to light
- Red spots inside the mouth with blue-white centers

Usually the spots will appear roughly two to four days before the rash shows up, giving you a clear indication of what your baby has.

Treatment

Many parents give their baby children's aspirin to treat the measles. Do not do this under any circumstances. Giving the baby aspirin when it has the measles can cause Reye's Syndrome, which is very serious and sometimes fatal because the disease causes fatty liver and swelling of the brain. Consult your doctor first before administering any medication. Usually, Ibuprofen is all right.

Treatment for measles is usually just to wait it out. Have your baby drink plenty of fluids, including water and fruit juice. Make sure your baby does not watch television because of their sensitivity to light.

To completely prevent the measles, you can get them vaccinated against the measles, mumps, and rubella with the MMR vaccine. Usually, this is given to babies aged 12 to 15 months. About 95 percent of all children who receive the vaccine will develop a complete immunity after the first dose. About 5 percent will receive their immunity after the second dose between the age of 4 and 6.

Sudden Infant Death Syndrome

Possibly one of the biggest worries of new parents is Sudden Infant Death Syndrome, or SIDS. The reason that many parents are so worried about SIDS is that there is really no answer as to why it happens. For infants aged 1-12 months, it is the leading cause of death, and every year 2,500 babies die from it in the U.S. There is no way to predict what babies will get it and what babies will not; that all being said, there are ways that you can reduce the risk according to some experts.

Even if your baby is perfectly healthy, it can strike and without warning. One merciful fact about this disease is that those infants who die from it show absolutely no signs of having suffered. Many die almost immediately. Usually, SIDS is diagnosed only after every other cause of death has been ruled out and the only explanation is SIDS. There are no single risk factors that cause some babies to be more likely to die from SIDS, and it strikes across the world in babies of varying health, sizes, and ages.

Typically, it will occur in babies aged two to four months. Oddly enough, there is a higher likelihood of a baby dying from SIDS in cold weather than in warm weather. African-American babies are twice as likely to die from SIDS, while Native-American infants are three times as likely when compared with Caucasian infants. In terms of the ratio between boys and girls, more boys will die from SIDS than girls, on average.

Potential risk factors according to SIDS experts, but which are not limited to, include:

- Mother smoking, drinking, or using drugs during pregnancy
- Premature birth
- Mothers younger than 20 years old
- Mother or father smoking near the baby following the birth
- Excessive sleepwear and bedding, causing the baby to overheat
- Baby sleeping on their stomach

Just because any of these factors may have occurred during the pregnancy or after it, it does not mean your baby may die from SIDS. However, many studies have shown that by ensuring your child sleeps on their back and not their stomach, it can help, hopefully, ward off SIDS.

While there is a lot of talk about SIDS, and while many parents worry about the disease, there is very little chance your baby will have it. Roughly 1 in 1,300 babies get it, which amounts to less than 1 percent of all babies in the U.S.

Other Diseases

The diseases we discussed above are by far the most common, but of course, there are many different kinds of diseases out there that can strike your baby. There is very little chance your baby will get these, but by preparing yourself, you can help keep your baby from suffering from these diseases.

Diphtheria

Caused by bacteria and spread by sneezing and coughing, this disease has mostly been wiped out in the western world but does still exist in some parts of the world, especially Africa, Central and South America, and parts of Asia. This disease starts with a sore throat and can move quickly to breathing problems. Eventually, the heart and nervous system will be damaged and death has occurred in some cases.

Tetanus

This disease still exists in the Western world, and tetanus germs that are found in soil spread it. Poisons are produced in infected wounds on the feet or hands that can cause problems with the muscles and eventually result in breathing problems. It is impossible to get this disease from someone else who has this disease.

Whooping Cough

Caused by bacteria, this disease is extremely contagious and is spread, not surprisingly, by coughing and sneezing. Babies can have this condition lasting for several weeks and can have bouts of vomiting and even choking. In some rare cases, this can be a fatal condition for your baby. Be sure to take your baby to the doctor if they begin to show symptoms of whooping cough.

Haemophilus Influenzae Type B

Found in the Western world, it is spread by coughing and sneezing and can be quite contagious. This disease will cause infection of the skin, problems with the lungs, blood poisoning, and even meningitis. If this disease is not treated quickly, it can become very dangerous for the baby.

Polio

While we usually think of polio as a disease that has been completely eradicated, this is not true. It still exists in some parts of the world and is spread by a virus that will attack the nervous system and cause permanent paralysis of the muscles. If the muscles in the chest become infected, it will usually result in death. Immunization in the Western world has nearly completely removed this disease as a threat to babies in the U.S.

Rubella

Often called German measles, it is a mild form of measles that is spread by a virus in saliva. It causes coughing and sneezing and is usually not a problem for babies or children. However, if the mother catches this while she is in early pregnancy, it can do harm to the fetus, and death can occur to babies who are born to mothers who have rubella.

Tuberculosis

This is another disease we think of as existing in the past, although it still affects thousands of people every year. When a baby is infected with this, it will cause coughing and problems with breathing. Children are not vaccinated for this until they are 10 to 14 years old.

Hepatitis B

This disease is passed by infected blood or through sexual contact if one of the partners is infected. Some people carry the virus but do not have the disease, and if there is an infection of Hepatitis B while a woman is pregnant, there is a chance she can pass that on to her baby. This will usually result in the baby becoming a carrier of the disease and developing it later in life. If you worry about this, your baby can get a vaccine within 24 hours of their birth that should prevent the development of the disease.

How Can You Prevent Illnesses And Disease?

Obviously, it is not possible to protect the baby from every disease, but by creating a certain type of home environment for your baby, it is possible to lessen their risk to disease, viruses, and bacteria.

Follow these tips to provide your baby with a healthy environment so that its immune system can grow strong in.

- If you are going to be visiting your child's doctor, it is important you give the doctor all the information relating to your child's health care. This includes:

- Tell the doctor your child's weight and whatever over-the-counter drugs they have taken.
- Tell the doctor about any dietary supplements the baby is taking, including all herbs and vitamins.
- Tell the doctor about any medication you are thinking of giving your baby.
- Ask the doctor about the drug they may be recommending, how long it takes to kick in, and what the side effects are.
- Tell the doctor the position that the baby is sleeping in.
- Give the baby lots of attention.
- Keep your baby away from too much exposure to the sun. Sunburns can be very painful and lead to other conditions down the line.
- Provide a safe environment for your baby.
- Do not smoke around the baby. No exceptions.
- Keep cleaning chemicals away from your baby, along with anything else that may be harmful to their health.

Conclusion

In a perfect world, your newborn would not get sick. Unfortunately, this is not a perfect world, and despite your best efforts, chances are your newborn will become ill, but that does not mean they are anywhere near close to dying. Throughout our lives, we get sick, recover, and get sick later on. It is just the way it is.

You have to remember that your baby is going to be exposed to a lot of germs, bacteria, and viruses. They have weak immune systems, they crawl everywhere, they touch everything, and they put everything into their mouths. It is simply a statistical probability that they are going to get sick from something.

The great thing is that when your baby does get sick, they will use their immune system to battle the virus or bacteria. That means that they will strengthen their immune system as a result. The more your immune system has to protect your body, the stronger it gets. We all want to keep our children away from anything that would make them sick, but doing this would actually hurt their health more than if you allowed them to get sick on occasion. The most important thing you can do is to ensure that you watch your baby and watch for symptoms. Do not worry about taking your baby to the doctor if you are worried. It is better to be too worried than not worried at all. The doctor can put your mind at ease and even prescribe something to make it easier on your baby and yourself.

CHAPTER 9

Baby Dangers

"Having a child is surely the most beautifully irrational act that two people in love can commit."

- Bill Cosby, American comedian

Previously in this book, we addressed how to baby-proof your home to protect your baby. This chapter, which will touch on that again because it is vitally important, is more about the dangers that lurk for your baby. While it may seem like the world is full of dangers and taking your baby anywhere or allowing them to move at all will just open them up to these dangers, the reality is that millions of babies live long and healthy lives. These days, many parents are overprotective because they worry about their babies. In the past, there was not this overprotective thought process, although parents were protective. They all turned out all right, so you should not be in a panic thinking that a new danger lurks around every single corner.

That being said, it is important to know the common dangers that exist for your baby so that you can ensure that it does not get hurt. Knowing these dangers allows you to plan for them while giving your baby the ability to grow and explore around the home and yard.

Most Common Cause of Infant Deaths

You should also keep in mind that accidents are not even in the top five causes of infant death. Here is a quick rundown of the causes of infant death according to the Center for Disease Control in 2003:

1. Congenital malformation or deformation   (5,621 deaths)
2. Low birth weight or premature birth   (4,849 deaths)
3. Sudden Infant Death Syndrome   (2,162 deaths)
4. Maternal complications during delivery   (1,710 deaths)
5. Placenta, umbilical cord, membrane complications   (1,099 deaths)
6. Accidents   (945 deaths)
7. Respiratory distress   (831 deaths)
8. Bacterial sepsis   (772 deaths)
9. Neonatal hemorrhage   (649 deaths)
10. Circulatory system diseases   (591 deaths)

Most Common Injuries Among Babies and Children

According to the National Safety Council (**www.nsc.org**), these are the most common causes of injuries among children and babies. We will touch on some of these in more detail later in the chapter.

- Falls
- Struck by or against something
- Overexertion
- Bites
- Stings
- Cuts
- Piercings
- Poisoning
- Motor vehicle occupant injury
- Bicycle injury
- Airway obstruction
- Fire or burn

Splitting this up, we see the most common injuries for children under the age of one, and children who are aged one to four.

Under the Age Of One Year

- Choking
- Motor vehicle occupant injury
- Drowning
- Fire or burn

Aged One to Four Years

- Drowning
- Motor vehicle occupant injury
- Pedestrian injury
- Fire or burn
- Choking

Now that we know the dangers, let us look at them more closely by addressing the various causes of these injuries. Knowing the causes of these injuries or accidents can better allow us to prevent them.

- **Choking:** Children love to put food in their mouths, but the problem is they do not always know what is food and what is not food. Children also love to test things through experimentation in their early lives and that involves testing thing by taste by putting the items in their mouths. We mentioned the toilet paper roll test to see if something can fit down your baby's air pipe, and it is important to do this test with anything you give your baby. Choking can occur due to a number of things lodging in the baby's throat. Some of the most common items that get lodged in throats include:
  - Buttons
  - Food
  - Beads
  - Coins
  - Pieces of toys
  - Hair ties
  - Pills
  - Foam
  - Pieces of balloons

Choking is something that children under the age of 3 are most at risk for.

- **Poisoning:** We live our entire lives surrounded by chemicals and poisons of all kinds. Our food is caked in pesticides, we use poisonous products to clean our houses, and that means there should be little surprise why so many babies die from poisoning each year. Beyond the obvious chemicals under the kitchen sink, poisoning in babies can occur from other things, including:
  - Eating a flower or plant
  - Taking too much medication
  - Sucking on glue
  - Eating a moth ball
  - Accidentally drinking alcohol

- **Burns:** It is surprising to think about the amount of hot things we have around us on a daily basis. We have stoves, microwaves, kettles, and coffee pots. We do not think much about them, but your baby might when it decides to investigate the new sensation of heat. Babies have very sensitive skin, and many burns are caused because parents do not think about that. Some causes of burns include:
  - Bath water that is too hot
  - Child turning hot water tap on
  - Heating of baby bottles and food in the microwave
  - Sunburns
  - Chemical burns from household products
  - Fireplaces
  - Stove tops
  - Heaters
  - Hot beverages on tables and counters

- **Electric shock:** Electricity is something we have a lot of but do not seem to think too much about. The truth is that electric shocks can be life-threatening. For babies, sources of electricity are curious things to investigate, but that can lead to premature death or injury. Some causes of electrical shock include:
  - Uncovered electrical outlets
  - Electrical appliances near water
  - Broken or frayed electrical cords
- **Fractures and head injuries:** Babies walk and stand, and when they do that, they often fall down. Sometimes they can fall against things or down things and suffer serious injuries. It is more common than you may think, and that is why it is very important to protect the baby from falling and hurting themselves seriously. Some of the more common causes of fractures or head injuries are:
  - Climbing furniture or pulling on furniture
  - Pulling on lighting like lamps that then fall on them
  - Falling down stairs
  - Falling against sharp edges
  - Falling off bunk beds
- **Cuts:** These are very common, especially if you do not always pick up everything that may get dropped. Our homes are full of areas that babies can cut themselves in, so it is important to watch for these dangers and prevent the injury before it can even happen. Some common causes of cuts are:
  - Broken glass
  - Sharp objects
  - Fingers getting stuck in door frames

- **Strangulation and suffocation:** The main cause of accidental infant fatalities under the age of one is suffocation. Suffocation can happen to babies when they have soft bedding or sleep on their stomach. It is important to remember that babies, especially newborns, do not move very well and cannot lift their heads, so if they sleep on their stomach there is the chance they will suffocate themselves with their face in the bedding. The more common causes of suffocation and strangulation are:
  - Babies sleeping on their stomach
  - Babies sleeping on pillows, cushions, comforters, or waterbeds
  - Drapes, blind cords, wall hangings with strings

  These are the more common causes of suffocation and strangulation, but there are some other lesser known causes as well. One cause of strangulation and suffocation is crib sheets that can be pulled up or pulled loose by the baby. Buying secure fitting sheets will prevent this, but poorly fitted ones can wrap around the rib cage or the neck of the baby. In 2001, *Good Housekeeping* did a study of 54 crib sheets and found that 47 of the crib sheets failed the test to see if they would stay secure with a baby pulling on them. All 47 could be removed with as little as ten pounds of force!

- **Re-breathing:** Many parents do not know what re-breathing is, but many experts feel it may be one of the leading causes of Sudden Infant Death Syndrome. Re-breathing involves breathing in carbon dioxide, which is dangerous to us in high quantities. When we breathe in, we take in oxygen but exhale carbon dioxide. Many trapped miners have died as a result of all the good air being used up and being replaced by carbon dioxide. When a baby sleeps on its stomach with loose or soft bedding under it, the carbon dioxide builds up around their head and face. This causes them to breath in the bad air rather than clean air. While most baby brains will tell them to move because they are breathing in bad air, some babies who may be predisposed to SIDS do not get that signal and end up suffocating.

- **Germs:** This is a harder one to safeguard against, but accidental ingestion of certain germs can cause babies to get very sick and possibly die. Bacteria and viruses are all around us, and while we have strong immune systems to fight the germs, babies do not. Even though they get immunities through breast milk, they are still at a greater risk for germs. This is why it is important to keep a clean house, do not let babies pick up things off the ground to eat, and to do baby laundry with the special instructions that come with it to prevent germ growth. Even taking your baby shopping can pose a risk. A study by the University of Arizona found that shopping cart handles, changing tables, and even restaurant tables have a high degree of disease-causing organisms that come from blood, mucus, saliva, and even urine; all that is left by those who used that table or cart before your baby started nibbling on it. Using hand sanitizers is a very good idea if you are going to be handling the baby a lot, especially after you have been out of the house.

Less Common Dangers

Surprisingly, there are dangers that are present in the things you buy especially for your baby, some of which are meant to help your baby in their early years. These dangers do not account for anywhere near as many deaths or injuries, or simple problems down the road as those above, but they should still be thought about before you purchase any.

Sippy Cups

Sippy cups are great for babies because they teach them to use a cup, and parents love them because there is no danger of spilling anything. However, dentists really hate these things because they contribute to tooth decay in babies and toddlers. When a baby or toddler uses a sippy cup, they are sucking the milk and juice directly to the back of their mouths, where bacteria collect on the back teeth. Many dentists feel that parents should just jump to letting the infant hold an actual cup on their first birthday, rather than moving to a sippy cup.

Baby Wipe Warmers

It is very uncomfortable for your baby to have a cold wipe applied to their bottom. It is a shock and not something they are going to enjoy. As a result, many mothers and fathers will go out and buy baby wipe warmers. What is odd is that these actually carry just as much of a risk of causing a fire as an electric blanket, and there is no chance you would think of putting your baby in an electric blanket. In the past ten years alone, three warmers have had to be recalled by the United States Consumer Products Safety Commission when it was found that cracks in the water tub caused water to come in contact with the electric components. Instead of using a baby wipe warmer, just use a warm cloth or heat up a wipe with your hands and your breath (as long as you are not sick).

Electrical Outlet Covers

It is very ironic that something you use to baby-proof your house could in fact hurt your baby. It is sad but true. The single electric outlet cover is usually a very safe product to have in your house, but there is the small chance that some small fingers may pop off one of those outlet covers that will not only expose the outlet but also create a choking hazard for the baby. Even forgetting to put the cover back on after using that outlet and leaving the outlet cover sitting on a table can lead to choking. These covers are more than small enough to fit in the toilet paper roll hole, so they can easily fit in your baby's throat. Instead of using this, look at getting a sliding plastic door cover that will cover the entire electrical socket.

Crib Decorations

Bedding sets with fluffy quilts, pillows that match, and a bumper may look good in the crib, but they can be dangerous for your baby. Many safety experts believe that these items can contribute to suffocation and SIDS, and that the crib should be empty except for spacers in the bars of the crib to prevent the baby's arms, legs, or head from getting caught in it. Putting the baby in warm clothing that cannot get tangled is a much better idea than putting in soft bedding that could tangle around the baby.

The crib slats that prevent the baby from putting their body through the gaps between the bars should be removed around five months of age when the baby is standing and learning that they can use those slats as something to stand on to get out of the crib.

To keep the baby sleeping in a certain position, many parents will buy a sleep positioner that keeps the baby sleeping on their back and not rolling over onto their stomach. Essentially, it is a piece of foam that fits over the baby's head and upper body. However, these can actually have the opposite effect for babies, rather than keeping them safe. Studies have found that babies can turn their heads from side to side within this foam casing, and since the foam molds to the face, it can actually cause suffocation.

Magnets

Magnets are actually very dangerous, especially refrigerator magnets that the baby can reach. These magnets can actually cause the baby to choke if they are swallowed. If by some chance the baby swallows two of them and they pass into the intestines, it is possible for the magnets to join together and cause a severe blockage that is often fatal.

Makeup

Makeup kits are easy to reach on an end table in the bedroom, and those nail polishes, eye shadows, lip gloss, and other forms of makeup carry several potentially toxic chemicals that can cause severe damage to internal organs if they happen to be swallowed.

Batteries

Batteries are not as much a choking hazard because it is possible for them to slide easily down through the throat. The problem arises when it gets into the stomach. In the stomach, it is possible for the batteries to begin leaking and even start shocking the baby from the inside. Never give a baby a toy that comes with batteries, as they will find a way to get the batteries out.

Conclusion

After reading this chapter, you may have the feeling that there is a danger around every corner for your baby. However, the point of this chapter was not to scare you or send you into a panic. It is only to help keep you aware of the various dangers that do exist for babies. It is also important to remember that many more babies die from unpreventable illnesses and problems than from accidents like choking.

Babies are born every day, and by far most of them survive through that difficult period of being an infant. The infant mortality rate in the United States is five out of 1,000, meaning only 0.5 percent of all babies born in the U.S. die each year.

Do not panic and do not worry; your baby is going to be just fine, and now that you know the dangers out there, you can prevent them from being a danger to your baby. That is part of what being a parent is all about.

CHAPTER 10

Games for the Baby

"There is nothing like a newborn baby to renew your spirit — and to buttress your resolve to make the world a better place."

- Virginia Kelley,
mother of former President Clinton

Earlier in the book, we talked about playing games with your baby. Here, we will give you more games that you can play with your baby that will help nurture your baby's mind and help them bond with you as their father (more on that in the next chapter).

These games are easy to play and require very little effort on your part, but they play a critical role in the development of your baby. Try to vary the games you play; that way, you keep your baby interested. These games will not help your baby if the baby is not interested in what you are doing. It will only make them irritable and cranky.

- Peek-a-Boo: The age-old game that helps your baby identify you. By just putting your hands over your eyes and then removing your hands and saying "peek-a-boo!" you will delight your baby for much longer than you would have expected.

- Helping your baby develop an understanding of their body comes from you singing, "Head and shoulders, knees, and toes" to them while you touch the parts of the body that you are singing about.

- Something as simple as a mirror can occupy your baby for hours. By putting them in front of a mirror while you make funny faces into it, you will not only be making your baby smile, you will be teaching them about recognizing themselves. This is a very important step in the baby's mental development.

- Since newborn babies have a stepping reflex, you can use this to your advantage. Just hold your baby up under the arms by grasping them firmly but softly around the chest. Stand the baby in the upright position on the floor. Whenever you lower your baby to the ground, their feet will lift up when they touch the ground. By shifting their balance, you can make it seem like they are walking. This reflex disappears around the age of two months.

- Babies are always trying to grasp something; it is in their nature and caused by their grasp reflex. You can use this to your advantage by laying the baby on its back and letting the baby hold onto your fingers. Then, gently lift their arm up and down as you say "up, down" so the baby begins to learn the concept of direction with this simple game. It will not be long before the baby begins to associate the words with the motion they are making.

- Put your baby on its back and rub their belly while you say "Rub a belly! Rub a belly!" After this, put the baby on its stomach gently and say "Roll over!" and roll them over. Keep doing this, and you will begin to find that your baby will begin to anticipate what you are going to do and will already start to move before you have a chance to move them.

- Babies spend a lot of time on their bellies as they begin to learn how to crawl. When they are on their bellies, they begin to develop strong back muscles that they will use later in the development for walking and sitting. Crawling around on the floor, around your baby, and playing games like "peek-a-boo" can be a lot of fun for the baby but a bit tiring for you.

- Imitation is a skill that babies begin to learn very early on in their development. This makes for a great chance to play some fun games with your baby in the first few months. Just put your face about one foot away from your baby's face, and when the baby is looking at you, do something like make a smile, frown, or just stick your tongue out. Repeat this facial expression every 20 to 30 seconds, and after a minute you should find that your baby begins to imitate your facial expression. This is a lot of fun for both of you and makes for great pictures.

- During the baby's first few months, they will be able to lift their head for a few seconds while they are lying on their stomach. If your baby is comfortable in this position, you can help strengthen their neck, arm, and leg muscles by rolling a brightly colored ball about two feet in front of them. The baby will concentrate on the ball as it goes by and even stretch to grab it. That stretch is like exercise, and it is important to give your baby lots of praise as they try to reach for the ball.

- Babies love to catch and grab at moving objects. All you have to do is attach a small stuffed toy to a bright ribbon and dangle it in front of your baby's face. Then, gently make the toy sway, and you will find your baby begins to reach out for the toy. When they grab it, give them lots of praise. If you can, use a squeaky toy because this will cause your baby to want to grab the toy even more. Doing this exercise will help to strengthen your baby's hand-eye coordination.

- Conversations are important in developing your baby's language skills. So, sit facing your baby, and begin to make baby sounds like "aaaah" and "baaaah." Before long, the baby will begin making the same noises, and the two of you will be having some great conversation.

- Bubbles are something that really interest babies. There is just something about these floating orbs that dazzle their eyes and hold their attention. You can take advantage of this by putting your baby in a bouncy chair or car seat and blowing bubbles around it. The baby will watch the bubbles as they move across its field of vision. One great aspect of this game is that when they touch the bubble, they will see it pop. This builds their cause-effect understanding by seeing the bubble pop on their touch. It will not take long before the baby begins touching the bubbles just to make them pop.

- Puppet shows are always a delight for your baby. By making some finger puppets with eyes, ears, and mouths, you can make them sing and dance for your baby. You can also make them kiss and tickle your baby as well. Your baby will be enthralled by this simple game and display of entertainment, and they will pretend the puppets are actually real. The great thing about that is it helps to develop their imagination at a very early age.

- As you will find out, babies love to dump things out. Whether it is your wallet, a box, a drawer, or any bag they come across, they will want to dump it out. You can make a game out of this by filling a plastic container with safe objects like stuffed animals and rattles. Just help your baby lift up the container and tip it over, and then show your baby how to fill it up again. Make sure you put objects of different sizes, shapes, and weights as well in the container. By doing this, you will help your baby develop the concepts of size and volume, which can help them with mathematics.

- Babies love to move when they start to become mobile. You can use this to your advantage for a great baby game. Just build a small obstacle course out of things like pillows and cushions. Encourage them to climb over the cushions and pillows to the finish line, where they get their toy.

- Around the age of nine months to one year, your baby may not be walking yet. If they are not, you can play a bit of kick ball with them by getting a lightweight ball and putting it in front of you. Then, hold your baby firmly under the arms, pick them up, and sway them gently forward so they kick the ball. You can help them kick this ball around by swinging their legs. The baby will have a lot of fun with it, and you will be helping to strengthen their stomach and leg muscles.

- Babies love to knock things over, and unless you want your alphabetized CD stack knocked over, you should give your baby an outlet for the need to bring things down. All you need are some lightweight books, empty cereal boxes, yogurt containers, and baby blocks. Stack them with your baby to create a tall tower. Then, when you are all done, you and the baby can start to take blocks out. Your baby will love seeing it crash, and they will also love trying out different shapes for the tower.

- Newborn babies can only see about ten inches in front of themselves. You can help improve their eyesight by taking a black and white object that you move around in front of them. Newborns cannot distinguish between colors, so a black and white object will work best. Move the object slowly, otherwise you may confuse the child. While you move the object, move it to a nursery rhyme tune. That way you help improve your child's hearing, vision, and even their understanding of rhythm.

- One game that will help you bond with your baby is to gently rock them with a gentle lullaby. You can even have your shirt off so that you can make skin contact, which is very important in the bonding process with you and your baby. The great thing is that newborns have an amazing sense of smell to make up for their poor hearing and eyesight at that age. They also have very sensitive skin. Therefore, by being that close to you, smelling you and hearing your voice and heartbeat, they will bond with you much better.

- Rattles are good for babies. They love the sound they make, and a rattle can be their favorite infant toy. With the rattle, you just need to sit close to your baby and shake the rattle back and forth in front of them. When you shake the rattle, make a surprised look and laugh when you hear the rattle make noise, then tap your baby's stomach. Keep doing this a few times and you will find your baby begins to anticipate the tapping of their belly.

- Mobiles are a great way to play with your baby and even watch them spend time by themselves. Mobiles play wonderful baby music, and the items that hang from the mobile can keep your baby's attention for a great deal of time. The colors will help them learn and distinguish colors, and the music will give them a good sense of musical rhythm early in their lives.

- With everything you do with the baby, sing a song. You can describe what you are doing, which does help as we have mentioned, but by singing a song with them, you help them learn about what you are doing in a fun way. Sing about changing the diaper, bathing, anything that you are doing while the baby is watching you. Even if the baby is not watching you, you will find they suddenly stop what they are doing when they hear you singing. Singing is something that seems to translate between ages, from baby to adult, and it is something that you can use to play with your baby and bond with them as well. When you sing, try and look in their eyes, as this will make the entire experience more enjoyable for your baby as they realize you are singing to them.

- Probably one of the most well-known and oldest forms of playing with your baby is with the song "Rock-A-Bye Baby." Just make your lap a cradle and lay the baby in it. Then, with a soothing voice, begin to sing the song to your baby as you gently rock back and forth. Ensure that you have the baby's head cradled while you gently rock them back and forth.

- Everybody loves a massage, especially babies. With some baby lotion, massage your baby's arms and legs. Gently move along their torso as you massage them. While you do this, make conversation with the baby about various things or what you are doing. You can even tickle them and blow on their tummy to get them to smile and laugh and make the massage more enjoyable for them. You should also try to massage your baby's face, moving your hand down the middle of the forehead, across the eyebrows, and down along the bridge of the nose to the corners of their mouth. The baby will be transfixed by this and will really enjoy the calming feeling of having you give them a baby massage.

- Roly Poly is a great game to play with your baby, and all you need is a beach ball or an exercise ball. Gently lay your baby on top of the exercise ball so that they are lying on their stomach. Make sure you firmly hold the baby's hips and gently roll them back and forth while you sing "Roly Poly." The baby will have a lot of fun with this, and you probably will to.

Conclusion

Bonding with your baby is very important, as we will look at in the next chapter. One of the best ways for you to bond with your baby is to play games with them on a daily basis. These are not games like Monopoly®, but more basic games that help the baby develop in a variety of ways. The games we have covered here help the baby bond with you and your voice, learn about rhythm, understand cause and effect, learn to think outside the box, see colors, and even strengthen their body and legs, which will help them later on in life when they begin walking.

Studies have shown that playing games with your child can help your baby later in life because of what they have learned in those early months. Babies are taking in so much from the world around them that it can seem overwhelming. By stimulating their minds, you will be able to help them make sense of the world around them and to develop a strong understanding about themselves and their place in the world.

As we will learn in the next chapter, bonding with your baby in this way will help foster a strong father-child relationship that will continue on for years to come and help the two of you have a great life together. When the baby identifies you as someone who takes the time to play with them and protect them, it can help in more ways than any of us truly realize.

Games can be fun for you as well. While the baby gets close to you, you can get close to the baby. You will be able to see their development as a person each time you play a game. It is surprising how happy it can make you to see your baby responding to you, making the faces you make and interacting with you. For so many months the baby was not totally a real concept. You knew you were having a baby with your partner, but that baby was hidden away in your partner. Now you can see the baby in front of you; you can see it moving and interacting with you. That realization fosters the bond with you and your baby, changing both of you forever.

CHAPTER 11

Being a Father

"And in that time, I lost my dad and had kids of my own. It was like, OK, I get it now. I know what fatherhood is all about. And you look at your parents differently."

- Paul Reiser,
stand-up comedian and actor

Understanding the relationship with your baby is very important. Bonding with your baby goes beyond just playing games. It involves showing your baby that you are there to care for them, protect them, and nurture them. You do not have to play peek-a-boo to accomplish this. You can find numerous ways to build the father-baby relationship.

Before you can understand the father-baby relationship, you need to look at yourself and ask yourself some questions about the baby and your feelings about being a father.

Can I Care for a Baby?

No one can know for sure if they are going to a good father. Of all the worries that hit new fathers, this is by far the most common. Thankfully, you are not alone in this. When you begin to wonder if you will be able to care for a baby, you can find solace in things like childbirth classes. Typically, you should be able to take classes with your wife as early as the 12th week of pregnancy. There are even classes that are meant for first-time dads to help them learn some of the things that you will need to learn to be a father.

Possibly the best thing about these classes is that you can meet other fathers who are going through the same thing. Being with fathers who are new dads is surprisingly reassuring. You will learn from them and what they have been told, and you can use your collective knowledge to help each other out. Many new fathers feel embarrassed asking experienced fathers questions about having a baby. You will not have to worry about that when you talk with new dads.

You are going to be a father, and you will be able to care for your baby. For generations upon generations, fathers have cared for sons and daughters. You will do the same, and you will do a fine job of it.

Will I Be a Good Father?

Probably the next most common question that you will ask yourself is if you will be a good father. Chances are you will care so much for your child that it will be nearly impossible for you to be a bad father. Look at it this way: If you are married, you probably asked yourself if you were going to be a good husband. Chances are now that you are a good husband, and you do not question it. The same is true with being a dad. You know how to treat children, what to do, and how to act, and that will come through with your own child. If you do worry, though, you can attend classes that will help you learn how to be a good dad. They will offer you resources about how you can care for your baby and how you can be the father you always dreamed about.

Talk with other fathers and find out how they worried about being a new dad and how they got through it. They can also tell you about some unexpected things that popped up and how they were able to deal with it. Other fathers can be your greatest resource when you have questions about the baby and about yourself.

Will I Be Able to Afford a Baby?

There is no denying that a baby is a huge expense. Babies will cost you a lot of money — thousands, in fact — within the first year. By the time they reach 18, you will have literally spent a small fortune on them through expenses like food, clothing, and school. So, will you be able to afford a baby? Chances are that yes, you will be able to afford a baby. The fact that you are worrying about this shows that no matter what, you will find a way to afford a new baby.

The first step in understanding the costs associated with a baby is to talk to your health insurer, employer, and your partner's employer to give yourself an idea of the initial costs of having a baby. You can find out from these people if you have paid paternity leave coming to you, rather than the standard unpaid maternity leave.

You should also look at talking to a financial planner who can help you by telling you what exactly you need to do to make sure your finances are stable after the baby arrives. They will tell you about some costs that may pop up that you did not think about. They can also help you for several years afterwards as the baby grows up. In terms of finances and babies, the financial planner may be your best friend.

One of the biggest expenses to do with children is college. Tuition costs continue to rise. In 2008, the average cost of a college education is more than $20,000, and in 20 years, it could be double or even triple that. Starting a college fund can help you save money for when your child is ready for college and keep you from taking a major hit with your expenses.

Will I Have Independence?

You probably asked yourself this question if you got married. You may think that being a father means there is no more fun in store for you. Well, you are wrong. In fact, fatherhood can be a lot of fun for you. It is true that you may not be able to go out whenever you want like you used to, or get a normal night's sleep in the first few months. However, as things begin to stabilize in the months after birth, you will find that many parts of your life will return to normal. This is why it is important that you talk with your partner and determine ways that the two of you can get time away from being a father or mother. This is very important because you will begin to find that the time you spend away from your partner and child is not as good as the time you spend with them. Eventually, your independence will be the last thing on your mind, despite the fact that you still have it.

You will be able to spend time with your child, teaching them and nurturing them. You can sit with them, talk with them, and play with them. You will love these times you spend together, and the small bit of independence you lost will be more than worth it for the joy that you get.

Can I Handle the Labor?

If the mother can get through the labor, so can you. Surprisingly, as tough as men make themselves out to be, many cannot seem to handle the birth. Many find it gross, and some do not even want to be in the delivery room. You need to be in the delivery room because your partner needs you there, and it is the least that you can do for her. However, you should remember that there is nothing saying you have to watch the baby emerge or cut the umbilical cord. You can simply stand next to your partner and help them get through the labor as easily as possible.

Childbirth classes can help out a lot with this. During childbirth classes, you will learn how to help your partner and know what to expect from the delivery process. You will be able to anticipate what is going to happen, and that will allow you to prepare for it. For many men, there is also the fear of fainting and the truth is that many men actually do faint in the delivery room. Most faint not because of what they see, but because of what they anticipate. Many think that there will be fountains of blood in the delivery room, when in reality there is much less blood — far less than they had anticipated.

Will I Be Able to Help My Partner?

Just like the worry of not being able to help the baby, there is the worry that you will not be as much of a help with your partner. This is not helped by the fact that your doctor may warn you that things sometimes go wrong during labor, and that there is the chance of health problems or birth defects for your partner and her baby. Naturally, this will worry you greatly and even set you with a bit of panic. This is why it is important to talk to experienced fathers about their own fears with their partner and how they got through it. Seeing the experienced fathers with their children and partner, who are all fine, will help to put your mind at ease.

While the doctor can be the bearer of doom sometimes, they can also help you understand the birthing process and what you can do to help your partner. They will answer the questions you have and limit the worries. Perhaps you worry about miscarriages because you have a friend who had three of them. You go and ask the doctor about it, and they tell you that there is only a small chance of miscarriage, and a slim chance of multiple miscarriages.

Helping your partner involves being there for her and not showing your worry. They need to see you as strong and able to be there for them. You will probably find as your partner gets pregnant that you cannot think of enough things to do to help her, and you will delight in getting her off her feet and treating her like a queen.

Issues for Fathers

As a father, you will go through various phases and deal with other issues as well. This is all normal, and you will be able to handle it accordingly. Here are some of the things that you can expect if you are a new father. Some of these may happen, some may not, but it is important to know about them:

Baby Blues

Mothers can experience post-partum depression, and fathers can experience something similar for the first few weeks after a birth. It is called the father's baby blues, and it is a period of low emotions, but it is much milder than what some mothers experience.

On occasion, some fathers will find that if they take time off work to be with the mother and child, they will have a lot of trouble getting back to work and being away from the family. This can lead them to become depressed. Furthermore, as we have mentioned, some fathers feel depressed and resentful over the bond between mother and child. They will want that same type of bond and will feel slightly left out if the bond is not as strong between father and child. It is important to remember as a father that you are helping your family by going to work, and that working provides the kind of life for your baby and partner that you want. Whether it is you or your partner working, or both, you both have the same end result of giving your child all the chances to succeed in life that you can.

Some fathers also feel resentful of the breast feeding, even though it is for the best with the baby getting all the nutrition that it can. In 1990, a study found that fathers are often concerned that they do not have the opportunity to develop a relationship with the child in the same way. This can cause feelings of inadequacy in the father, which leads to baby blues.

Add in the pressure of the finances on the father when they go back to work, and you have a clear cause of why some fathers become depressed for a period after the baby is born.

The good thing is that this depression passes, usually when the fathers begin to bond with the baby and see the baby's smiling face each day.

As a father, if you want to feel more involved with the breast feeding and develop that same bond with your child, you can do the following:

- When it is time for breastfeeding, bring the baby to the mother.
- Settle the baby down after they have had a feeding with the mother.
- Cuddle with the mother and child during the feeding.
- Burp the baby after they have finished breastfeeding with the mother.
- If the baby falls asleep while they are breastfeeding, which does happen, you can wake up the baby.

Being a Primary Caregiver

The change that will come with being a new father will be most apparent during the first few days when the baby is brought home. During the first few days, you will be the primary caregiver for both the mother and child. You will be helping your partner through the day after the exhausting work of childbirth, and you will be helping the baby almost completely until your wife is ready after recovering.

This period of being the primary caregiver can be quite a bit longer if your partner has a C-section. For her, the recuperation period will be much longer and more painful than if she had a traditional birth. You will need to not only monitor your partner's health, but also help her if she begins to suffer from post-partum depression.

Bond With the Baby

The best time to bond with your baby (apart from bonding their entire lives) is to bond during the first few weeks. You may have never held a baby, dealt with a crying baby, changed a diaper, or knew that a baby's head is shaped oddly after a birth, but that should not stop you from bonding with it as much as possible.

This can be difficult because usually the mother has more time to bond with the baby than you do in those first few weeks, but it is important that you find time to bond with the baby. On top of that, you need to bond with the mother as well, showing that you care deeply for her and the baby. If she is suffering from post-partum depression, this will help her get through the condition.

How to Bond With the Baby (Beyond Games)

- When the baby is in the womb, talk to it. We went over this earlier in the book and we mention it again because it is such an important part of the bonding process. According to a study by Queens University, babies are able to distinguish voices that they hear by their 30th week in the womb. Babies can pick up father's voices very easily because males have deeper voices that are easier to hear in the womb. This same study found that if the father speaks to the baby in the womb, the baby is more receptive and able to recognize the voice of their father after they are born. Whether it is singing, talking, or just reading to the baby in the womb, it all helps in the bonding process.

- Ask the mother to provide you with space for a little time each day so you can bond exclusively with the baby. This way, you can bond with the baby without the mother, which is important. You should bond with both of them no doubt, but by bonding with the baby exclusively for a little each day, you will have a better ability to become closer to the baby. Do not worry about your partner being offended by this. In fact, she may jump at the opportunity for a few hours by herself after weeks of catering to the baby whenever it needs something from her.

- Usually mothers take their babies shopping with them, but it is also a good idea for you to take your baby shopping using a sling-type carrier. This way, you can bond with the baby while carrying them close to you. Physical closeness is a very natural way to bond with your baby. You can use this same type of carrier any time in the day to keep your hands free. You can go for walks with the baby, nap with the baby, and even do the dishes while you are holding the baby like this.

- Diaper changing is a great way to bond with your baby. It may be messy, sometimes gross, but that closeness fosters a strong bond with the baby. You will change hundreds of diapers over the course of your life, and by helping to shoulder part of the workload of your partner, you bond with your baby and strengthen your relationship with your partner.

- Along with sharing the workload of diaper changes, you can also share the tasks of feedings and sleeping. If you feed with the bottle and breast, then you can handle the bottle duty while your partner takes care of the breastfeeding. Splitting up feedings gives you both the opportunity to bond with the child.

- Give the baby a sponge bath.

- If the mother is busy, take the baby to the doctor during their scheduled checkups.

- Rock the baby to sleep to help develop a strong bond with the baby as it falls asleep.

- Dressing the baby is also a great way to get close with the baby, while at the same time accomplishing the task at hand.

- Earlier in this section, we mentioned participating in the birth. In terms of bonding with the baby, this is very important. Talk with your partner and ask if you can be the first to hold the baby in your arms and to make eye contact. Doing this, along with cutting the umbilical cord, can bond you to the baby forever.

- Whenever you can, even if it is during bath time, you should make skin-to-skin contact with your baby. This is simply an excellent way to bond with the baby, and it is also an easy way to get the baby used to the bathtub. With you in the bathtub with them, the bath can become a soothing place, which will help you down the road when you are telling your child that it is bath time.

- Dancing is not only fun, it is a good way to bond with your baby, whether you are holding the baby in your arms, or have it strapped to your chest with a sling carrier. The baby likes to be moved around, and it is also a good way to soothe the crying. Sometimes, you can even get the baby to fall asleep with this, while you bond with them at the same time.

- The outdoors is a great place to be, and it is a great place to take your baby. Go for a walk or a jog with your baby. The baby will fall asleep as you push them in the stroller, and you will both be able to breathe some fresh air.

- Cuddling with your baby as you nap on the couch is a good idea as well, as long as you do not move around in your sleep. You should not cuddle or co-sleep with your baby if you have epilepsy, an infection, or if you smoke.

- The baby likes silly things and that means you can be silly, too. Making faces and silly noises, blowing on their tummy, or just sticking out your tongue will bond you with the baby. You get to be silly, and no one says anything!

- Making eye contact with your baby is very important. There is a connection that develops when you cradle the baby in your arms and look at them. Simply put the baby at chest level and look into their eyes. The baby will be transfixed by your stare, and you will feel bonded with them as well.

- When the baby was in the womb, you may have decided to play music for it. You should continue with this even after the baby has been born. Play fun music for the baby, including lullabies and nursery rhymes. Singing with the baby and dancing with it will help you both bond with each other.

- Midnight bottle feedings are the perfect opportunity for you to bond completely with your baby. By doing the midnight bottle feeding, you give your partner a break. With no distractions, no television, and just the quiet of the night, it is the perfect time to be bonding together. It may be late, but you will find that you begin to look forward to the midnight feeding as a great bonding experience with your baby.

- Just because you have a baby does not mean that you cannot enjoy the sports page. The baby does not care what you read, so why not sit back and read the baby the sports page. You never know, you may cause the baby to develop a strong attraction to sports, something that you may really enjoy later in life.

- Once the baby begins to eat solid food, you can begin to have dinners with it. If your partner is out, or if she is just resting, you can begin having dinners for two with your baby. You can enjoy your dinner while the baby enjoys their dinner. They may play with it, throw it, or just stare at it, but the point is you are spending time with the baby, and that is always important at this early stage.

- You do not want your baby to be sick, but when it is, you can begin to bond with it. Rocking the sick child can help calm the baby down if it has a cold or fever, and it can help you bond with the baby when it is most vulnerable.

- If you enjoy working out, then having a child means you have a new set of weights to work out with. This is great because going to the gym might not happen as much as you would like because of the baby, but because babies weight as much as 20 pounds, you can build your muscles while still playing with the baby. You can only do this when your child's neck can support the weight of their heads. Balance the body on your palms and ensure your fingers are curled around it. Then, slowly move them up and down as if you are bench pressing them. You will get a good bit of exercise, and some babies absolutely love this.

- Babies love texture, as we have mentioned, and you have plenty of textures on you. If you have a beard or just stubble, let the baby feel the hairs. They can feel the smoothness of a mustache, or the sharpness of stubble. They can play with your hair and even pull on it. Just be careful that the baby does not grab your chest hair; they are surprisingly strong when it comes to grasping things.

- Take pictures of your baby. You will love being able to capture the early life of your pride and joy, and your baby will love the extra attention they are getting from you. Just remember that babies are sensitive to bright lights, so try not to use the flash very much.

- When the baby gets a bit older, around six to 12 months, you will be able to roughhouse with it. You should never shake the baby in any way, but you can hold the baby when they are old enough to sit up and very gently toss them in the air and catch them. You can also bounce them on one knee, or even cradle them like a football. It is a great way for you to bond with the baby and have a good time with them as well.

Conclusion

Being a father is a new experience that you may or may not be ready for. In fact, you may find it to be a very frightening prospect if you have not experienced it before. Being a new dad, though, can be a great experience. You can learn more about yourself, your baby, and your partner. You can get closer to your family and create a bond that will last your entire life. There are many questions that you will ask yourself, some of which can be answered, and there are many things you will have to address about yourself before and after the baby arrives.

Will you be a good father? Will you be a caring husband? Will you have the money to give the baby the life you feel it deserves?

It can be hard to answer these when you have no frame of reference in your life to go on, but the truth is that you will not know until you try, and once you do, you will find that not only were most of your worries unfounded, but that you cannot imagine your life without the bundle of joy you now have.

Being a father is one of the greatest journeys you will ever have in your entire life.

CONCLUSION

From this point on, there will be a little life that depends on you and needs you. It will look to you for guidance, it will look to you for protection, and you will be there to provide it to your child.

Many new fathers will say they have the fear of losing their independence, of being a good father, and of being able to care for something like a baby. These are common worries, and they are needless worries. You will be able to care for a baby, just like millions of other fathers around the world are able to care for their own babies. It is part of our nature to know how to care for our babies and to help them grow to adults to become functional members of our society.

From the moment your partner tells you that she is pregnant, to the day the baby is delivered, you will be going through changes in your life that may seem overwhelming. You may panic, you may worry, but you will also be excited about the baby that is coming and the amazing change that is going to happen. You will see something you helped to create growing in your partner. You will be able to experience this miracle of life with her throughout those nine months. While you may have anxiety or worry during that time, those feelings will be trumped by the excitement you feel.

Once the baby is born, you will suddenly have the realization that there is something that needs you and depends on you. From the moment that the baby opens its eyes and looks at you, you will be forever bonded to it. Whatever you may have thought beforehand, all you will think about now is of that little bundle of joy in your arms.

You will be able to teach that child about the world around them, play with them, and help them grow by nurturing and bonding with them. The time you spend away from your child will be nearly unbearable and the time you spend together will be time you cherish for the rest of your life. You will not even remember the worries you had as you play with your baby, show it off, and brag about the progress it is making.

A baby is a big step, but it is often a step in the right direction and a step that will leave you changed forever. From this point on, you are a father. You are one of the caregivers of a new life, a life that will look up to you for guidance and help. You will find that you will feel like people need you throughout the pregnancy and the first years of your baby's life. Your partner will need you during the pregnancy because she will be going through some pretty extreme but amazing changes, and she will need you there to support her and help her. After the birth, you will be helping your partner through the stages of birth and the time after delivery. At the same time, you will be working and nurturing the new life that has entered your life. It is an amazing time and possibly the first real moment where you realize that being a father is a lot of fun and a life-changing experience as well.

Congratulations, you are about to take an amazing journey: The journey of fatherhood. There is no other journey that can compare to this!

SECTION 4

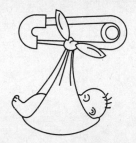

Appendices

APPENDIX 1:

Glossary

Courtesy of www.achildtolove.com/terms

A

Abortion: The termination of the pregnancy before 20 weeks. This is the voluntary abortion of the fetus, not the involuntary (that is often known as a miscarriage).

Alpha-Fetoprotein (AFP): A plasma protein produced by the yolk sac as it grows within the uterus.

Amino acids: The building blocks of the embryo and fetus.

Amniocentesis: This is the removal of fluid from the amniotic sac. This fluid is then tested for genetic defects.

Amniotic fluid: This fluid surrounds the baby that is within the amniotic sac or womb.

Amniotic sac: The sac that surrounds the baby within the uterus.

B

Back labor: Pain in the lower back caused by the weight of the baby in the front of the body.

Biophysical profile: Evaluating the baby after birth by the doctors to ensure proper breathing, heartbeat, and other tests.

Blastomere: A cell the egg divides into after it has been fertilized.

Braxton-Hicks contractions: Painless tightening of the uterus that is irregular.

Breech presentation: Buttocks or head of the fetus coming out first during labor.

C

Cesarean section (C-section): Delivering the baby through surgery by removing the baby from the abdomen.

Colostrum: The first milk to come out of the breast, usually yellow and thin and completely harmless to the baby.

Congenital problem: A genetic problem with the baby that can be seen after birth.

Conjoined twins: Twins that may share vital organs and are connected by a part of the body, like the abdomen and head.

Contraction stress test: The response to contractions to determine the well-being of the fetus.

D

Developmental delay: A condition where the development of the baby is slower than normal.

Dizygotic twins: Twins that come from two different eggs. This is usually called fraternal twins.

Dysplasia: Abnormal changes in the cells of the cervix.

E

Ectodermic germ layer: This is the layer of the embryo that produces the skin, teeth, mouth glands, nervous system, and pituitary glands of the fetus.

Ectopic pregnancy: Pregnancy that occurs abnormally outside the uterine cavity, usually within a fallopian tube.

Embryonic period: First ten weeks of fetus gestation.

Endodermic germ layer: The layer of the embryo that produces the digestive tract, respiratory organs, vagina, bladder, and urethra.

Endometrial cycle: This is the development of a membrane that serves as the lining of the inside of the uterus.

F

Face presentation: When the baby emerges from the birth canal head-first.

Fallopian tube: Tube that leads from the cavity of the uterus to the area of the ovary.

False labor: Thinning of the uterus without dilution of the cervix.

Fertilization: Sperm and egg joining.

Fertilization age: Two weeks before the gestation age. This dates the pregnancy from the point of fertilization.

Fetal anomaly: An abnormal development in the fetus.

Fetal goiter: An enlarged thyroid on the fetus.

Fetal monitor: Used during labor to listen to the heart beat and vital signs of the baby.

Fetal period: Time after the embryonic period that lasts from the tenth week until birth.

Frank breech: Buttocks extending first during the delivery.

G

Gestational age: Dating age of pregnancy from first menstrual period.

Gestational diabetes: A worsening or beginning of diabetes during the pregnancy.

H

Habitual abortion: Three or more miscarriages.

Human chorionic gonadotropin (HCG): Early pregnancy hormone. It prevents the disintegration of the corpus luteum. This is crucial because it maintains the progesterone production during pregnancy.

Human placental lactogen: Placenta hormone that is produced during pregnancy and found within the bloodstream.

I

Immune globulin preparation: Used to protect against a variety of diseases during pregnancy.

In utero: Inside the uterus.

Inevitable abortion: A pregnancy with severe complications including cramping and bleeding that will most likely lead to a miscarriage.

J

Jaundice: The staining of the skin, eyes and tissues of the body so that it has a yellow color to it.

L

Laaoo: Expelling the fetus from the uterus.

Lightening: The changing in the shape of the pregnant uterus a few weeks before delivery. This is sometimes called baby dropping.

M

Mask of pregnancy: A butterfly shaped pigmentation that can appear under the eye of the pregnant woman.

Meconium: The first intestinal discharge of the newborn that consists of cells, mucus, and bile.

Missed abortion: A miscarriage without bleeding.

Mittelschmerz: Pain that happens when the egg is released from the ovary. The pain is centered in the pelvic or abdominal area and usually only affects 20 percent of women.

Monozygotic twins: Identical twins conceived from one egg.

Morning sickness: Vomiting and nausea during the first weeks of pregnancy, not associated with any sort of ill health.

N

Neural-tube defects: Abnormalities in the development of the fetus' spinal cord and brain.

O

Oligohydramnios: A deficiency of amniotic fluid.

Omphalocele: An out pouching of the umbilicus that contains the internal organs of the fetus.

Ovulation: Regular production of an egg from the ovary.

P

Paracervical block: Anaesthetic for cervical dilatation.

Pelvimetry: Using X-Ray to determine the size of the birth canal and the pelvis of the mother.

Phosphatidyl glycerol: A lipoprotein that occurs when the lungs of the fetus mature.

Placenta: An organ that is attached to the baby via the umbilical cord.

Placenta accreta: An organ that attaches to the uterus muscle.

Placenta increta: An organ that grows into the muscle of the uterus.

Placenta percreta: A placental organ that enters the muscle of the uterus.

Placenta previa: A low attachment of the placenta.

Placental abruption: The separation of the placenta that is premature.

Placentamegaly: A large growth that occurs during the pregnancy in the placenta.

Premature baby: When a baby is born before 37 weeks of gestation.

Postnatal blues: A mild depression caused by hormonal imbalances after the birth of the baby.

Postpartum depression: A deep depression caused by hormonal imbalances after the birth of the baby.

Postpartum hemorrhage: Bleeding more than 15 ounces at the time of delivery.

Presentation: How the baby appears as it comes out of the vagina during birth.

Q

Quickening: The baby moving within the uterus.

R

Round-ligament pain: Pain that is caused by stretching ligaments in the uterus.

Rupture of membranes: The breaking of the water when fluid breaks through the amniotic sack, signifying labor is beginning.

S

Spina bifida: A defect in the vertebral column caused by the incomplete closure of the embryonic neural tube. This results in a spinal cord that has formed incompletely.

Spontaneous abortion: The loss of pregnancy during the first 20 weeks of pregnancy.

Spotting: Light bleeding that is common during the first trimester of pregnancy. This may resemble a light period.

Station: The estimated descent of the baby. Estimation of the descent of the baby.

Stretch marks: Red marks on the skin that occur when the skin is stretched.

T

Threatened abortion/miscarriage: Bleeding during the first trimester that is heavier than spotting.

Transverse lie: A fetus that is turned sideways within the uterus.

Trimester: The three equal time periods of the pregnancy during which various development occurs.

U

Umbilical cord: The cord that connects the baby with the placenta. It removes waste and CO_2 from the baby, and provides the baby with oxygen and the nutrients it needs to grow.

Ureters: Tubes that drain urine from the fetus

Uterine atony: A lack of tone within the uterus.

Uterus: The organ that the fetus grows in during pregnancy.

V

Vacuum extractor: Used to help provide traction on the baby's head during the delivery if there is a problem with the baby coming out.

Varicose veins: Enlarged or dilated blood vessels.

Vertex: Head first delivery.

Z

Zygote: Cells that are created when the sperm fertilizes the egg.

APPENDIX 2:

Popular Baby Names

Courtesy of Social Security Administration (www.SSA.com),
"Most Popular Baby Names."

Most Popular Baby Names of 2008

	Male	Female
1.	Jacob	Emma
2.	Michael	Isabella
3.	Ethan	Emily
4.	Joshua	Madison
5.	Daniel	Ava
6.	Alexander	Olivia
7.	Anthony	Sophia
8.	William	Abigail
9.	Christopher	Elizabeth
10.	Matthew	Chloe

Most Popular Names of the 20th Century

	Male	Female
1.	James	Mary
2.	John	Patricia
3.	Robert	Linda
4.	Michael	Barbara
5.	William	Jennifer
6.	David	Elizabeth
7.	Richard	Margaret

8.	Joseph	Susan
9.	Charles	Dorothy
10.	Thomas	Betty
11.	Christopher	Nancy
12.	Daniel	Karen
13.	Donald	Lisa
14.	Paul	Helen
15.	George	Jessica
16.	Mark	Sarah
17.	Matthew	Sandra
18.	Kenneth	Donna
19.	Steven	Carol
20.	Edward	Ruth

Most Popular Baby Names in 1880

	Male	**Female**
1.	John	Mary
2.	William	Anna
3.	James	Emma
4.	Charles	Elizabeth
5.	George	Minnie
6.	Frank	Margaret
7.	Joseph	Ida
8.	Thomas	Alice
9.	Henry	Bertha
10.	Robert	Sarah

Most Popular Baby Names in 1900

	Male	**Female**
1.	John	Mary
2.	William	Helen
3.	James	Anna
4.	George	Margaret
5.	Charles	Ruth
6.	Robert	Elizabeth
7.	Joseph	Florence
8.	Frank	Ethel
9.	Edward	Marie
10.	Henry	Lillian

Most Popular Baby Names in 1910

	Male	Female
1.	John	Mary
2.	James	Helen
3.	William	Margaret
4.	Robert	Dorothy
5.	George	Ruth
6.	Joseph	Anna
7.	Charles	Elizabeth
8.	Frank	Mildred
9.	Edward	Marie
10.	Henry	Alice

Most Popular Baby Names in 1930

	Male	Female
1.	Robert	Mary
2.	James	Betty
3.	John	Dorothy
4.	William	Helen
5.	Richard	Margaret
6.	Charles	Barbara
7.	Donald	Patricia
8.	George	Joan
9.	Joseph	Doris
10.	Edward	Ruth

Most Popular Baby Names in 1950

	Male	Female
1.	James	Linda
2.	Robert	Mary
3.	John	Patricia
4.	Michael	Barbara
5.	David	Susan
6.	William	Nancy
7.	Richard	Deborah
8.	Thomas	Sandra
9.	Charles	Carol
10.	Gary	Kathleen

Most Popular Baby Names 1970

	Male	Female
1.	Michael	Jennifer
2.	James	Lisa
3.	David	Kimberly
4.	John	Michelle
5.	Robert	Amy
6.	Christopher	Angela
7.	William	Melissa
8.	Brian	Tammy
9.	Mark	Mary
10.	Richard	Tracy

Most Popular Baby Names 1980

	Male	Female
1.	Michael	Jennifer
2.	Christopher	Amanda
3.	Jason	Jessica
4.	David	Melissa
5.	James	Sarah
6.	Matthew	Heather
7.	Joshua	Nicole
8.	John	Amy
9.	Robert	Elizabeth
10.	Joseph	Michelle

Most Popular Baby Names 1990

	Male	Female
1.	Michael	Jessica
2.	Christopher	Ashley
3.	Matthew	Brittany
4.	Joshua	Amanda
5.	Daniel	Samantha
6.	David	Sarah
7.	Andrew	Stephanie
8.	James	Jennifer
9.	Justin	Elizabeth
10.	Joseph	Lauren

Most Popular Baby Names in 2000

	Male	Female
1.	Jacob	Emily
2.	Michael	Hannah
3.	Matthew	Madison
4.	Joshua	Ashley
5.	Christopher	Sarah
6.	Nicholas	Alexis
7.	Andrew	Samantha
8.	Joseph	Jessica
9.	Daniel	Taylor
10.	Tyler	Elizabeth

BIBLIOGRAPHY

Wikipedia Article, 'Pregnancy'
http://en.wikipedia.org/wiki/Pregnancy#Physiology

Wikipedia Article, 'Morning Sickness'
http://en.wikipedia.org/wiki/Morning_sickness

Wikipedia Article, 'Ultrasound' http://en.wikipedia.org/wiki/Ultrasound

CTV.ca, "Caffeine Doubles Miscarriage Risk, Study Finds," Jan 22. 2008
www.ctv.ca/servlet/ArticleNews/story/CTVNews/20080121/caffeine_
miscarriage_080121?s_name=&no_ads=

Wikipedia Article, 'Maternity Leave'
http://en.wikipedia.org/wiki/Maternity_leave#Americas

LoveToKnow.com, 'Cost of Having a Baby,' Gallup, Betsy
http://pregnancy.lovetoknow.com/wiki/Cost_of_Having_a_Baby

'Soothing music reduces stress, anxiety and depression during pregnancy
says study,' Oct. 6, 2008, Wiley-Blackwell www.alphagalileo.org/ViewItem.
aspx?ItemId=2848&CultureCode=en

HowToDoThings.Com, 'How to plan a nursery you will love,'
www.howtodothings.com/family-relationships/how-to-plan-a-nursery-
you-will-love

www.dol.gov/esa/whd/regs/statutes/fmla.htm

Wikipedia Article, 'Cesarean,' http://en.wikipedia.org/wiki/Cesarean

BabyCenter.com, 'Buying and Installing a car seat,' www.babycenter.ca/baby/safety/carseatinstall/

WikiHow Article, 'How To Change A Diaper,' www.wikihow.com/Change-a-Diaper

Googobits.com, 'Boost Your Baby's Brain Power,' Aug 12, 2005, Templeton, Rita www.googobits.com/articles/2113-boost-your-babys-brain-power.html

FamilyEducation.com, 'Redesigning your life as a parent,' http://life.familyeducation.com/parenting/discipline/36652.html

BabyCenter.com, 'Managing stress and anxiety during pregnancy,' www.babycenter.com/0_managing-stress-and-anxiety-during-pregnancy_1683.bc

Wikipedia Article, 'Baby Colic,' http://en.wikipedia.org/wiki/Baby_colic

Suite101.com, 'Baby games for four to six months: Playing with your growing infant,' July 30, 2007, England, Angela http://baby-todler-play.suite101.com/article.cfm/baby_games_for_four_to_six_months

Suite101.com, 'Baby games for seven to nine months: Playing with your growing infant,' July 30, 2007, England, Angela http://baby-todler-play.suite101.com/article.cfm/baby_games_for_seven_nine_months

Suite101.com, 'Baby games for nine to twelve months: Playing you are your growing infant,' July 27, 2007, England, Angela, http://plantsbulbs.suite101.com/article.cfm/games_for_nine_to_twelve_months

BabyCenter.com, "Development Milestones: Walking,' www.babycenter.ca/baby/development/walking/

Government of Saskatchewan, 'How to talk with your baby,' www.health.gov.sk.ca/talking-with-your-baby

BabyCenter.com, 'Introducing Solid Foods,' www.babycenter.com/0_introducing-solid-foods_113.bc?page=1

'Top 5 Teething Tips,' March 20, 2006, Bradley, Nicki, http://baby.families.com/blog/top-5-teething-tips

ParentTime.com, 'When babies are cutting a new tooth: Tips for parents on soothing infants through the discomfort of teething,' www.parenttime.com/babyarticles/teethingtips.html

MayoClinic.com, 'Teething Tips,' www.mayoclinic.com/health/teething/FL00102

BabyCenter.com, 'Parents' top potty training tips,' www.babycenter.ca/toddler/pottytraining/parentstips/

KeepKidsHealthy.com, 'Potty Training Resistance,' www.keepkidshealthy.com/parenting_tips/potty_training/potty_training_resistance.html

BabyTalk.com, 'Common Baby Illnesses,' www.baby-talk.co.uk/illnesses.htm

KidsHealth.org, 'SIDS,' http://kidshealth.org/parent/general/sleep/sids.html

TenderBabyCare.com, 'Baby Care,' www.tenderbabycare.com/

Canoe.ca, '7 toy dangers you should not overlook,' Toffelmire, Amy http://chealth.canoe.ca/channel_section_details.asp?text_id=4158&channel_id=145&relation_id=16285

AOL.com, 'Top five most surprising baby-product dangers,' Bradford, Stacey L., http://money.aol.com/top5/general/worst-baby-product-buys

EzineArticles.com, 'Baby dangers new parents need to know about,' Mullen, Sharon, http://ezinearticles.com/?Baby-Dangers-New-Parents-Need-to-Know-About&id=30459

About.com, 'Top 10 leading causes of infant death,' June 21, 2007, Morrow, Angela. http://dying.about.com/od/causes/tp/infantdeath.htm

Pettit, Paul and Pam, 'Congratulations, You are Gonna Be A Dad!', Kregel Publications, 2002

Brott, Armin A., Ash, Jennifer, 'The Expectant Father,' Abbeville Press, 2001

Downey, Peter, 'So You are Going To Be A Dad,' Simon and Schuster Australia, 2000

Greenberg, Gary, Hayden, Jeannie, 'Be Prepared: A Practical Handbook for New Dads,' Simon and Schuster, 2004

SSA.com, "Most Popular Baby Names," **www.ssa.gov/OACT/babynames/**

AUTHOR BIOGRAPHY

Craig Baird is a writer based out of rural Canada, where he
lives on a ranch with his wife and dogs. He has published
several books and short stories, as well as written for
magazines and newspapers across Canada. When he is
not writing, he spends his time traveling the country and
hiking in the outdoors with his wife, Layla.

INDEX